Free Elections

In the same series

In Preparation

Free Elections

AN ELEMENTARY TEXTBOOK

BY

W. J. M. MACKENZIE

Professor of Government
The Victoria University of Manchester

GEORGE ALLEN & UNWIN LTD
Ruskin House
Museum Street London

Printed in Great Britain
in 10 point Plantin Type
by John Dickens & Co Ltd
Northampton

ACKNOWLEDGEMENTS

My thanks are due in the first instance to the Government of Tanganyika and to the University of Khartoum, the University College of East Africa and the University College of Rhodesia and Nyasaland, for the invitations which suggested the preparation of this book. Its completion would not have been possible without the assistance of Mr. Peter Campbell, of Manchester University, on whose immense learning and generosity all his friends rely. Needless to say, none of these are responsible for the opinions expressed in this book, or for its errors and limitations.

I must also thank Mr. John Foley, M.B.E., of the Electoral Registration Office of the City of Manchester, for his kindness in explaining practical details of administration in the constituencies for which he is responsible: to my former secretary, Mrs. Kathleen Ashton, for her speed and patience in dealing with a difficult manuscript: to Mr. H. W. Harris, for his indispensable help in preparing the index.

W.J.M.M.

The Victoria University of Manchester
November, 1957

CONTENTS

PART THREE: ADMINISTRATION AND ADJUDICATION

PART FOUR: ELECTORAL MORALITY AND ITS ENFORCEMENT

CHAPTER I

Introductory

This book is the result of the author's experience as a visitor to East and Central Africa in the years 1952 and 1956. In the first year the idea of self-government based on an electoral system giving representation to all sections of the population was so strange that it was a matter of some delicacy even to discuss it publicly. By 1956 it had become axiomatic that this was the next step in progress, and there was lively controversy over the mechanism of elections in all the British and ex-British territories from Khartoum to Salisbury: the Sudan, Uganda, Kenya, Tanganyika, Zanzibar, the Rhodesias and Nyasaland. This preoccupation with one aspect of the problem of self-government at first seems odd, but it is not illogical. The only consistent answer offered by the West to the problem of legitimate power is that government must be based on free elections. The problem of elections is therefore central, and its importance extends far beyond East and Central Africa. A question of the electoral system, that of the inclusion of 'coloured' voters on the same voting roll as 'whites', has been the symbol of the struggle for predominance between Afrikaner and British ideas of government in South Africa. In India and in West Africa the introduction of direct elections with universal franchise has been the badge of nationhood; questions about elections stand in the path of further progress in many other colonial territories (Malaya and Singapore, Mauritius, British Guiana among others), as well as in the countries of French North and West Africa, and the new states of South East Asia.

Indeed, the problem is not merely one of colonial self-government. The catchword 'free elections' has become a badge of the difference between two ways of life reckoned to be in antithesis. Some people in the West object to the economic policies of communism, and believe they should be fought at all costs. But there are many others who would accept the proposition that a government is entitled to try what economic policies it likes, provided that it is a government truly representative of the people. This follows, after all, from the Western doctrine of the self-governing nation-state. But when is a government 'democratic'? To Marxists, if it is based on the leadership of the only 'democratic' party, the Communist Party: to the Western democrats, if it is based on 'free elections'. But when are elections 'free'? No election

11

can be wholly free, because unlimited freedom of choice negates itself: it is impossible that each elector should choose his own candidate, and an attempt to do so would merely throw the government into the hands of the best-organised minority. Freedom in elections is not an absolute, but a gradation: at what point on the scale are we to say that 'freedom' has been attained?

This sort of question presents logical difficulties, but there is no great difficulty in practice in recognising 'freedom', or an advance towards 'freedom', so long as we understand what sort of thing the scale is. This question about the scale of freedom is not a straightforward one, because electoral systems are built out of a number of different elements, which react on one another, so that a change in one direction may be balanced by a change of opposite tendency elsewhere: but it is one which it is possible to answer. There has been much experience of electoral systems which are normally reckoned to be 'free', and from this experience emerges some knowledge which can be set out in a systematic way. It is odd that, so far as the author is aware, this has not yet been done. There are many simple text-books on other parts of the constitutional structure of democratic government, such as parliamentary procedure, federalism and local government, the organisation of the public services: but there is no general description of the elements of a free electoral system.

This book is an attempt to fill that gap. It attempts to describe electoral systems in general, not one electoral system in particular. To some extent such a description can be based on deduction from first principles; there are some problems which *must* arise wherever the attempt is made through elections to put a choice of candidates before a very large number of voters. But first principles do not take one very far, and much of what follows consists of generalisations from the practice of electoral systems which have admitted defects but are both stable and free; 'stable' in the sense that one election has succeeded another without violent breach of continuity for many years, and also 'free', in that the issue of the election depends on the voters' choice. This means, in fact, generalisation from the experience of Britain and of those Dominions in which electoral systems have taken root successfully; the U.S.A.; France; and the smaller Western democracies. No attempt is made to describe any of these systems specifically, but reference will be made to them where it seems helpful for explanation.

It should be added that the main emphasis here is on elections to central legislative assemblies, and that very little is said about two other kinds of election, the election of officials and the election of local councils, or about voting in plebiscites and referenda. The greatest of all elected officials is the President of the U.S.A., and an American presidential election is the greatest electoral show on earth, so great that in the U.S.A. it dwarfs Congressional elections altogether. It is also important to realise that in a developed democratic system the election of local councils interlocks with the system of legislative elections, so that they form part of one political structure. It is never possible to keep national politics out of local government; but where local government is strong, national politics may take on a special character because they are anchored to the rock of local interests, and because the careers of politicians depend on success in sponsoring and mediating between such interests. Presidential elections and local elections may therefore in particular circumstances be of extreme importance; they are omitted here only because discussion of them would lead beyond the first principles of election.

The method of this book is intended to be objective and technical. It deals to some extent with questions of values and of success in achieving them: but the author's main object is to indicate the range of choice which is open, the arguments which can be used one way or the other, and the consequences entailed by different lines of action. It is unlikely that the result will be uncontroversial: personal preferences are bound to peep through. But after 500 years' experience of these matters there ought surely be a good deal of ground common to all observers; and if bias appears here the fault is the author's.

There are, however, other matters which cannot be discussed without certain presuppositions, and it may be best to explain two sets of assumptions which will reappear later in the book, sometimes explicitly, sometimes by implication.

First, what is the object of 'free elections'? Some may say that they are an object in themselves, or (at least) that free government is an object in itself. 'Let there be free elections though the heavens fall.' This is a powerful doctrine, which the author cannot accept without qualification, for two reasons: first, because it is wise (as modern philosophers point out) to 'cash' such general statements into specific proposals before assenting to them, and this book illustrates only part of the complexities which arise when one proceeds to 'cash' the ethical doctrine of the goodness of free government; secondly, because though free government (whatever exactly it may be) is certainly a 'good', it is not the only 'good' that men seek or ought to seek, and the complexities of balance between ultimate ends involve issues too deep for this book.

Without digging so far, one may still maintain that free elections though not a supreme end are yet a device of the highest value, because no one has invented a better political contrivance for securing in large societies two conditions necessary for the maintenance of government in any society. First, elections can create a sentiment of popular consent and participation in public affairs even when government is so complex as to be beyond the direct understanding of the ordinary citizen. Secondly, elections can provide for orderly succession in government, by the peaceful transfer of authority to new rulers when the time comes for the old rulers to go, because of mortality or because of failure.

There may be occasions when the rulers must take responsibility upon themselves: there are extremities which require the old Roman proclamation of executive rule—'let the consuls see to it that no harm comes to the Republic'. But the doctrine of responsibility to an electorate is the best for ordinary use, because it is the only available guarantee of consent and continuity in government.

It is not, however, a guarantee which always works; the world is strewn with the wreckage of electoral systems. What then (secondly) are the conditions under which it is prudent to introduce free elections? It is assumed here that there are four conditions which are ideally necessary. There are (first) an independent judiciary to interpret electoral law; (secondly) an honest, competent, non-partisan administration to run elections; (thirdly) a developed system of political parties, well enough organised to put their policies, traditions and teams of candidates before the electors as alternatives between which to choose; (fourthly) a general acceptance throughout the political community of certain rather vague rules of the game, which limit the struggle for power because of some unspoken sentiment that if the rules are not observed more or less faithfully the game itself will disappear amid the wreckage of the whole system.

These are of course ideal conditions, never completely realised anywhere, and never likely to be realised; but in large societies government through free elections is only possible if some advance has been made towards them. Conversely, if it is intended to introduce free elections in a country not accustomed to them, it is essential at the same time to build the conditions of free elections, and so to handle elections at first that they do not accentuate weaknesses and retard development.

This leads to a final point. The introduction of free elections is a difficult political undertaking, the rules of success are not precisely known, the risks of failure are great. Why take such risks? The answer is that we cannot help it. Peoples seeking free government can advance only by following the model given by those who claim already to possess it. The demand for freedom grows by opposition, and can be checked only by natural disasters or by repression so violent as to cripple economic life. Concession therefore is inevitable, and, once begun, the process of concession is accelerated by its own momentum. Only one thing is certain, that each country has its own political life, and that old institutions will work differently in a new setting. Whatever happens in the end to the doctrine of free elections, the result will be very different from the system which grew up in Western Europe and was spread over the world by European emigration and European domination of colonial territories. The system has its own logic independent of history, but its practice is historical, marked by the idiosyncracies and internal contests of various Western nations; its future value depends on the possibility of adaptation in countries where this Western history means very little.

Part One: Voters and Candidates

CHAPTER II

The Voters
General Qualifications and Disqualifications

1. *Introductory*

Any code of electoral law includes a number of essential sections of almost equal importance; these deal with the qualifications and disqualifications of voters, the method of voting, the division of the electorate into constituencies, the prevention of corruption and intimidation during the campaign, the judicial and administrative provisions for seeing that the law is observed. Each of these sections is meaningless in isolation from the others. A very wide and equal suffrage loses its value if political bosses are able to 'gerrymander' constituencies so as to suit their own interests: there is no point in having an elaborate system of proportional representation if the electors are all driven in one direction by a preponderance of bribes and threats; legal provisions mean nothing if enforcement of the law is left wholly in the hands of those who profit by breaking it.

This is why it is right to speak of 'the electoral *system*'. Procedure for elections is *systematic* in that its parts are inter-dependent; it is impossible to advance on one 'front' without regard to others. Similarly, exposition in a book is difficult because there has to be a good deal of cross-reference between sections. But one can have no election at all without voters, and it seems best to begin by talking about qualifications for the vote.

This may, however, be misleading. The school histories of electoral reform in England in the nineteenth century emphasise the extension of the suffrage by stages from 1832 to 1928, and this was the aspect of reform which appealed most to ordinary men and women at the time—'Will I get the vote?' But the politicians who passed the Reform Acts thought just as much about the distribution of voters into constituencies: after all, each constituency that exists is the 'seat' of some politician, and it would be exquisitely painful if it were snatched from under him. The working of English politics was modified as profoundly by the sum of detailed changes in some 600 constituencies, as by the dramatic introduction of new electoral qualifications. There is some risk that to put 'voters' first here may encourage self-deception about this; extension of the suffrage has great popular appeal, but it may be so 'worked' as to produce unexpected results.

2. General qualifications

It is convenient to divide qualifications for the franchise into two
sections, general and special. The reason for this is that there must
always be some limitations on the franchise, even under 'universal
suffrage'. Suffrage is the basis of government within a political community; therefore, it rests on a definition of membership of that
community.

Babes in arms cannot vote, if the system is to be taken seriously;
therefore, there must be some specification about age. Are women
political animals at all ? In some parts of the world this remains an open
question; and there must therefore be a general decision for or against
discrimination according to sex. What importance is to be attached to
affiliation to a locality within the territory ? Some evidence of affiliation
is essential, because each holder of a vote must, in order to cast it, be
attached to one constituency and not more than one constituency. [1] But
should more than the bare minimum of attachment, that of presence in a
constituency on a qualifying date, be required to show that the voter
does in some real sense 'belong' to the constituency in which he votes ?

(a) *Citizenship.* It is generally taken as a matter of course that only
citizens of a country may elect representatives to its public bodies.
This is the rule, but it admits of certain curious exceptions:—

(i) There was a period in the nineteenth century when in some states of
the U.S.A. immigrants could be registered as voters after a very short
period of residence in the country, a period too short for the acquisition
of citizenship. This was partly the result of competition for votes
between political parties; but in an expanding country it had a certain
rough justice about it. Why should the weakest of all the inhabitants,
the new immigrant from Ireland or from the Jewish Pale of old Russia,
be weakened still further by refusal of the vote ? Circumstances have
changed, and the American states (on which franchise in the U.S.A.
depends) are now as strict as other countries in insisting that the vote
follows citizenship, which requires five years' residence.

(ii) The development of the British Commonwealth has led to the
evolution of a peculiar sort of citizenship law by which citizens of each
independent country of the Commonwealth possess by mutual arrangement the status also of 'British subjects and Commonwealth citizens'.
The 'mother country' is now in law an equal member of the Commonwealth, under the name of 'the United Kingdom and Colonies', and it
has its own special citizenship. This 'citizenship of the United Kingdom
and Colonies' can be acquired very easily by citizens of other Commonwealth countries who come to live in Britain; but in spite of this, there
is no rule that they *must* acquire this United Kingdom citizenship

[1] There are a few exceptions, below p. 107.

before voting in a United Kingdom election. Any citizen of any country in the Commonwealth can vote in Britain if he is present here on registration day and is otherwise qualified, even though he is not a citizen of the United Kingdom and Colonies. This privilege is extended, for historical reasons, to citizens of the Republic of Ireland, which is not now a member of the Commonwealth.

(iii) There is generally in colonial territories advancing towards self-government a puzzling stage when a start has to be made with elections, although the territory concerned does not yet possess a citizenship law of its own. For instance, the bulk of the inhabitants of Nigeria or Northern Rhodesia or Tanganyika have the status either of 'citizens of the United Kingdom and Colonies' or of 'British Protected Persons', not that of citizens of their own country, since no 'local citizenship' yet exists. Similar, and perhaps more difficult, problems arise in Malaya and Singapore. Therefore, to introduce the franchise in territorial elections, one must first *either* pass a law about territorial citizenship *or* take a decision within the franchise law about the people who are to be deemed 'real' inhabitants of the country for the purpose of voting in it. The latter course, if it is chosen, may decide the basis of citizenship later, because it is hard first to give a man a vote, later to tell him he is not a citizen and take it away.

In this situation there are three variables that can be used: birth in the territory; length of residence in the territory with proper legal authority; possession of some other status such as that of 'British subject and Commonwealth citizen', 'British protected person', or 'citizen of the United Kingdom and Colonies'. These variables admit of many permutations and combinations, which perhaps do not need fuller explanation. There will always be a balance of theoretical arguments between (on the one hand) generous extension and (on the other) strict insistence on evidence of close attachment to one country to the exclusion of others; in most cases, the decision also has effects on the result of elections, because it affects the proportion of people of different political tendencies to be enfranchised. An extreme instance of this is the position in Northern Rhodesia, where there is at present a 'common roll' franchise limited to British subjects, which thus excludes virtually all African inhabitants of the territory, since their status is that of 'British protected persons'. A change of the electoral law in this one respect would constitute a very important decision about the basis of politics in Northern Rhodesia, unless counteracted by some other change.

(b) *Age*. It is usual to look for a legal definition of 'full age' (varying in different countries from eighteen to twenty-five), as used in some other context, and to adopt this definition for the purposes of the electoral law. If the electoral age is cut loose from the recognised age of maturity, awkward arguments ensue, prompted sometimes by calculations about the political affiliation of particular age groups. In 1918 the United Kingdom brought the voting age for many men down to nineteen for one election only, by giving the vote, at that age to those who were serving in the forces, or had served, 'in connection with the present war': in the same year, the compromise clause enfranchising women did not admit them to the vote until the age of thirty, lest the party system be swept away by a sudden majority of women voters.

Two minor matters may affect the decision about age, without raising any issues of principle.

(i) In many countries registration of births is still imperfect, and it is hard to prove age satisfactorily. Fortunately, however, these countries usually impose certain obligations at a given age, such as military service or the payment of adult poll-tax, and the individual therefore possesses some document giving evidence of the date when he was called up or first paid tax. Age admitted to his disadvantage can fairly be used as evidence to his advantage when he claims a vote.

(ii) The fact that a vote is given by law at the age of twenty-one to all otherwise qualified need not mean that these young men and women can vote if there is an election the day after their twenty-first birthday. There may well be a time lag before their names can be placed on the electoral register, a matter dealt with more fully in §3 (c) of Chapter XIII.

(c) *Sex* (perhaps) is not a matter which admits of compromise. The effects of enfranchising women may be mitigated (if that is the object sought) by altering other qualifications; by the differentiation of age referred to above, or by making the vote dependent on evidence of payment of tax, in countries where few women are liable to tax. But the decision itself is a straight decision, 'yes' or 'no'; a rare thing in arrangements for the franchise.

(d) *Local affiliation* (as has been explained earlier) must be defined in order to secure a closed list of the voters who are entitled to make the choice of member or members within a territorial constituency. There are some extreme cases in which birth in the constituency is either a required qualification or an alternative to residence, for instance in the electoral regulations of 1955 in Western Nigeria; or a distinction may be drawn between temporary and permanent residence, as in the 1956 regulations for African elections in Kenya. At the other extreme are provisions of a purely formal kind, necessary to decide the allocation of electors between constituency registers, a matter referred to again in §2 (c) of Chapter 13. A small instance from the United Kingdom will illustrate what is involved. In England, Scotland and Wales it is enough that as an elector should be resident in a constituency on the registration day; the law used to specify a longer period, which disenfranchised a certain number of people who were for some reason migratory, but this vanished in 1918. But an Act of 1949 restored a qualifying period of three months' residence for registration in any constituency in Northern Ireland; this was done because there was a slight risk that the balance in some marginal constituencies there might be upset if additional voters could be brought across the vexed Border in large numbers to establish residence with friends for a day or two at the time of registration.

3. Disqualifications

Every qualification entails a disqualification, and *vice versa*, but there are some general qualifications which it is natural to put negatively. There are minor variations in practice in different countries, but there are only two points which have caused much controversy.

(i) It is usual to disfranchise persons certified to be lunatics or mental defectives.

(ii) It is almost equally usual to disfranchise convicted criminals serving their sentences in prison.

(iii) It is a common provision that temporary or even permanent disqualification for voting should follow conviction for certain electoral offences, either automatically or at the discretion of a court.

(iv) In eighteenth-century England the votes of government employees might be decisive in some of the very small constituencies where there was a concentration of dockyard workers or customs officials, and reformers attempted to weaken the government's control over these boroughs by disfranchising certain categories of officials. Customs officers were disfranchised in England until 1868, police constables until 1887. This is not a matter which is likely to be important now, since the votes of officials, or even of members of the armed forces, are rarely numerous enough to affect the decisions of large modern electorates.

(v) One does, however, still find instances of the Victorian argument in favour of disfranchising paupers and tax defaulters. This is the reverse of 'no taxation without representation': no representation for those who draw more from the state in cash than they contribute to it, no representation for those who default in the civic obligation to which representation is related. Both arguments belong to the days when special emphasis was laid on the 'cash nexus' in society; we have come so far from this now that even the name 'pauper' is unknown, and we all take some cash benefits from public funds. It is possible to sympathise with the officials (particularly in local elections) who dislike noting as one of their masters a man from whom they have tried unavailingly to collect an acknowledged debt: but the system of disqualifying tax-defaulters has acquired a bad name because of the use of poll-tax as an instrument of disfranchisement in the Southern States of the U.S.A. This is a tax (now used less and less) which the officials do not make any attempt to collect: but no one can be registered as a voter unless he has paid poll-tax some time in advance of the registration date. Naturally, only voters organised by the dominant party remember to pay their tax in time.

A word should perhaps be said of the type of disqualification which was in force in Russia from the 1917 revolution until the Stalin constitution of 1936. Franchise was then refused to all members of the former governing class; persons employing hired labour for the sake of profit, those living on unearned income, private business men, monks and clergymen, employees and agents of the former police, and members of the former ruling dynasty in Russia. This was a consistent application of a system of ideas which is not that of 'free elections'. The regime was in principle a regime of dictatorship of the proletariat, in alliance with the peasantry and revolutionary intelligentsia, led by the Communist Party on the basis of its knowledge of the true science of society. Given these premises, it was logical to disqualify members of former governing classes so long as they presented a danger to the regime, and to remove the disqualification when these classes had become so weak that they were no longer a danger. Some of the disqualifications were so expressed that exact legal interpretation of them was difficult; and in practice it was a matter for the Party, through local electoral commissions, and not for an independent court, to say whether an individual *bourgeois* or his sons and daughters had purged their class origin by 'socially useful work'. There was a similar practice during part of the Revolution period in France, and doubtless examples are to be found during disturbed periods in many countries. An extreme example is that of the African franchise law of 1956 in Kenya, which did not permit a member of the Kikuyu, Embu and Meru tribes to register, although otherwise qualified, unless he could show to the satisfaction of a District Commissioner that he had actually aided the administration during the Mau Mau troubles.

CHAPTER III

Special Qualifications

1. *The Arguments*

It is convenient to begin, not by classifying special qualifications, but by explaining the arguments used to justify them. There is a risk that this may be misleading, because such qualifications are adopted in practice as a result of political struggle and compromise, and theoretical arguments are only one factor, and perhaps not the most important, in decisions about the franchise. But so much ingenuity has been (and will be) spent on finding special qualifications to suit special local circumstances that it is impossible to describe them all; whereas the arguments involved are simple and well-worn, and may give some coherence to a confusing subject.

There is (first) a watershed between the arguments which assume that certain persons have in some sense a general or 'natural' right to vote, superior to the interests of the state in which they vote and not dependent on its laws; and those which assume that the vote is a privilege or responsibility, given by the legislation of the state in the interests of the state or of the community as a whole. There is, however, a deeper division here in principle than in practice, because there are some important practical consequences which can be deduced alternatively from either theory, so that both theories can be used to defend them.

(a) *The vote as a right.* The first theory has taken various forms at different periods:—

(i) It may be said that the state rests on the consent of all adults, freely associated together, and that therefore there should be universal and equal adult suffrage (for men and—sometimes—for women too), subject to no limitations except those required for the successful administration of the system.

(ii) Or it may be said that the state rests on property, and that the right to vote belongs basically to holders of property, either in goods or (the strictest version of the doctrine) in land. This is the 'stake in the country' theory, characteristic of eighteenth-century and early nineteenth-century England.

(iii) It is sometimes claimed that the state exists to serve the interests of a particular class or race or social grouping, which alone has the right to representation in the government. This may lead to the Russian conclusion quoted above, that all but proletarians, peasants and revolutionary intelligentsia should be disfranchised, and to the further conclusion among those enfranchised the votes of proletarians should count for much more than for those of peasants; or to the conclusion reached in South Africa or in the old South of the U.S.A., that only whites are entitled to vote for the supreme authority, because the state is in its nature a white state.

(b) *The vote as a privilege.* From the second theory, that of the overriding interest of the state, it is also possible to deduce a variety of conclusions:

(i) It is possible to justify equal universal suffrage on this ground also. The argument would usually (though not necessarily) run as follows: The object of the state (it is said) is to maximise the happiness of its people. This total happiness is the sum of the separate happinesses of all the individuals concerned, and no one is better qualified to look after the interests of an individual than the individual himself. He may of course fail, through weakness, ignorance, or folly: but it is even more likely that his interest will be betrayed if he has no power to guard it himself. Hence the best, perhaps the only, security for the general interest is to give the vote to each individual as a weapon with which to protect his own interest.

(ii) It may be replied to this that it is optimistic to expect wise policy to emerge from the sum of individual ignorance and simplicity: and that the interest of the state can only be secured if the voter is treated as a person responsible not only to himself but to the public as a whole. In voting (it is maintained) a voter discharges a public office: he should look to the interests of the whole, not to his own interest alone. If this is accepted, it follows that the state is entitled to scrutinise the suitability of the voter for the discharge of his office; voters should be chosen because of their worthiness, and worth may be a matter either of character or of skill. This line of thought has been the main justification for special qualifications (or 'fancy franchises', as they were called in Victorian England), and much political debate has turned on rather unreal arguments about the character and skill of voters.

(iii) A third view of the situation is that voters and their representatives are (and should be and can only be) primarily spokesmen of interests. The King (or the government) summons Parliament in order to ascertain the thoughts and wishes of 'all sorts and conditions of men'; what is wanted in a legislative body is not remarkable wisdom or unselfishness but the capacity to speak effectively for all the diversity of interests which together make up the national interest. It is for the assembly to debate, for the government to listen and to reconcile. This argument was used in a subtle way to justify the extreme complexity and confusion of the old British electoral system, which was first given some uniformity in 1832. It can also be used to justify a franchise so devised as to ensure that important 'interests' are not squeezed out of an assembly by sheer numbers. This may lead to a 'weighting' of the franchise in favour of minority interests; or to the introduction of separate electorates for separate interests (a matter referred to again in Chapter IV); or to the use of other devices, such as the manipulation of constituencies (Chapter XII), or the use of special forms of voting (Chapter VII, §3).

None of these arguments is quite without substance; but there is not much doubt that in the conditions of the twentieth century the force of argument (as well as the force of events) tends towards suffrage which is both universal and equal. There are various reasons for this. The case is a pretty good one in itself, both on ethical and on practical grounds. As a matter of political tactics, it is a case which is irresistible in its appeal to large bodies of men, and if universal suffrage is not conceded the demand for it becomes a convenient slogan behind which many interests not otherwise connected can rally to upset the government. The arguments in favour of a specially selected electorate grow weaker with the growth of mass literacy and the techniques of mass communication. Above all, universal suffrage has been tried in many different societies, and the disasters prophesied before the event have on the whole not followed.

It is not therefore possible today to enter upon discussion about free elections except on the assumption that they must ultimately rest on equal adult suffrage, and on the sort of administrative and party organisation which this entails. But adult suffrage is relatively new in the West, and so is equality. Manhood suffrage was reached in France and in the U.S.A. about 1850, in most Western European countries by 1900, in Britain by 1918, universal suffrage including women was not reached in the whole of the U.S.A. until 1920, in Britain until 1928, in France until 1944. In Britain plural voting—the giving of an extra vote or votes to special classes of voters—was of little importance once virtually complete adult male suffrage had been reached in 1918: but it survived in a limited form until the University degree vote and the business premises vote were abolished in 1948. There was therefore a fairly long period during which were built the other institutions which make equal adult suffrage workable, and the best argument for special qualifications at present is that they may in some countries be necessary as an interim measure to allow for 'running in' a new political and administrative machine during a difficult period of transition.

2. Some Varieties

From this point of view special qualifications can best be set out under three headings, property (or income), education, status. Under each heading, very many sub-divisions are possible, and varieties can be multiplied by combining sub-divisions in different ways. But in any given situation the choice is strictly limited by considerations of practice. There are two over-riding requirements which will appear repeatedly in this book: first, that the administration should be able to settle the entitlement of voters, prepare electoral registers and run the election effectively with the resources of staff and time at its command, without letting all other administrative business go by default; secondly, that the rules about the qualification of electors are precise enough to admit of quick and impartial decision even at a time of intense political excitement. Special qualifications must be precise and simple, or they will not do, even as a transitional device.

(a) *Property or income.* There is no point in discussing here the level to be set for property or income qualifications; this is a matter of local circumstances and local bargaining. It is, however, of general importance to remember that property or income qualifications can only be expected to work easily if they are related to some assessment made independently of the process of elections. Registration officers cannot be expected to act as valuers, except in a situation (like that under the Kenya African elections law of 1956) in which no one expects serious pressure from voters to get their names on the roll. Property qualifications worked reasonably well in Britain for some four hundred and fifty years because they were tied to a universal form of public assessment for tax. Income qualifications in British territories always meet the difficulty that the income tax authorities are strictly bound by tradition not to make public the incomes of individual taxpayers. These difficulties can in most places be avoided, given patience and ingenuity; but the result may be that some holders of quite large property or income are excluded from the franchise because they hold it under communal tenure or in some other way that precludes individual assessment.

(b) *Education.* An educational qualification may be anything from bare literacy to the holding of a university degree or higher professional qualification. Once again, the details are matters of local bargaining; but a somewhat similar general point arises. In a society which is moving forward rapidly into the conditions of the modern world, the most natural form of educational qualification is that of literacy, either in any language or specifically in the 'language of culture' within the territory. This fits in with the general arguments for a 'quality franchise', because it brings in those most directly within the zone of modern 'mass communications', and encourages by political recognition a qualification which is necessary to the advancement of society. Besides, it may be fairer to use literacy as a test than to require evidence of formal education, because the educational system is new and expanding, and to insist on formal tests penalises older people who have taught themselves, in favour of the young who have at least spent some years at school.[1]

The other side of the account is that literacy tests have become notorious for their use in certain countries as devices for securing other objects indirectly, as for instance the exclusion of Asiatic immigrants from Australia. In quiet conditions an administrative officer can decide pretty quickly by simple tests which of the applicants who came to him are to be judged literate; and on the whole they will accept his judgment so long as it appears unbiassed. But simple literacy tests are extremely vulnerable to political pressure. Politicians may incite voters to wreck the tests, either by faking literacy or by lodging so many appeals that the system is likely to collapse. Or they may seek to control the administration of the tests, so as to exclude their opponents from the voters' roll. This leads to the conclusion that where there is a real political fight in progress an educational qualification must be based on some certificate given independently of the electoral administration. This may be very hard on the 'late learners', but nothing can be done for them except to invent some special 'adult literacy' examination giving a qualification not primarily intended for use in elections.

(c) *Status.* This discussion of property and education has led to the conclusion that workable qualifications under these heads may squeeze out many people who would be thought 'worthy' to vote, if the argument from quality were taken seriously. Hence there is a search for other criteria; and in colonial territories this is encouraged by the sentiment (general among the 'old guard' of administrators and settlers) that tests based on cash and on education tend to select the wrong sort of worthiness, because they disregard the sterling qualities of experienced men and women still living within a traditional society, where property is held in common and formal education is unknown. Many different criteria are suggested: holding office as a chief or tribal elder; membership of a local council; long service and good conduct in some employment; seniority by age; the possession of a certificate as a good farmer; and so on. Such qualifications are not objectionable in principle so long as they do not rest simply on appointment by the administration, but they are not easy to set out in a form sufficiently precise to admit of independent assessment. At best they may be of value to smooth out anomalies and maintain a balance between the old society and the new during a transitional period. Experience suggests, however, that in practice traditional authorities stand their ground in their own localities, but are ready to accept the leadership of new men in national business of a new kind; so that the counterpoise against domination by the forces of rapid change is more apparent than real.

[1] Almost unavoidably, a pure literacy test disfranchises blind persons.

3. *Single or plural votes*

Such special qualifications may be alternative or cumulative. That is to say, voters may be allowed only one vote,[1] even though they are qualified under more than one heading; or they may be allowed to gain additional votes by qualifying under several headings or at a higher level under one heading. To take an example of these latter variants:—

(a) The 'Coutts' franchise, introduced for Africans in Kenya under the African elections law of 1956, lists special qualifications for men under seven headings. A man obtains one vote if he qualifies under one heading, two votes if he qualifies under two headings, three votes (the maximum) if he qualifies under three or more headings.

(b) The English Poor Law Amendment Act of 1834 deliberately restricted the election of those responsible for administering poor relief to owners of land and ratepayers in the parish concerned; and weighted the vote still further in favour of property by giving extra votes up to a total of seven in proportion to ownership of lands, up to three in proportion to rateable value of property occupied.

If plural voting is allowed it can be organised in two quite different ways:

(a) The plural voters may vote in the same constituencies as other electors, simply having more votes to cast and thus more influence on the result. Here again there is a sub-division:—

(i) The plural voter may have several votes in one constituency, as in the old Poor Law Board elections in England.

(ii) He may not have more than one vote in any one constituency: but may vote in more than one ordinary constituency if he is qualified by tenure of property in several places or otherwise. This was the nineteenth-century British practice in Parliamentary elections. Rich electors who had more than one vote could vote in a number of different constituencies, so long as elections were spread over a period of several days; but the effects of plural voting were reduced by the Act of 1918, which enacted that all constituencies should poll on the same day, and forbade any elector to vote in more than two constituencies at a general election, and it was finally abolished in 1948.

(b) Plural voters may be given their second (or further) votes in special constituencies of their own. The most famous instance is that of the British constituencies of University graduates, which lasted from 1603 until 1948, returning at their highest point 12 members in a House of Commons of 615. The similar device of a 'graduates' constituency'

---

[1] Except in a multi-member constituency with simple plurality voting (*see* Chapter VII, § 1), when the 'single voter' has as many votes as there are members to be elected.

was used in the Sudan elections of 1948 and 1953, although in this case 'graduates' meant all who had completed secondary education; in 1953 there were five 'graduate' seats in a House of 97, and this seems to have had an important and probably beneficial influence during the period of transition, as it imposed some concentration of effort on the small class of educated Sudanese, who might otherwise have been submerged in tribal and religious politics. This system of special constituencies is only one step from that of plural or communal electorates discussed in the next chapter.

The case for plural voting is primarily that it is a simple way of giving extra weight to voters whom the state wishes to favour. It is possible to differentiate in favour of 'skilled' and 'responsible' voters by giving them extra votes, and yet to bring into the system a fairly wide range of voters who have only one vote each. Without plural voting the same bias can only be given by excluding this 'lower' level of voters from the franchise altogether. A secondary argument is that if a second vote is given to special classes of electors (such as University graduates) in separate constituencies it has the effect of diversifying representation by requiring a rather different type of campaign and selecting a different type of member. This may happen even where there are not separate constituencies, provided that the 'second votes' are geographically concentrated; that is what happened in the old City of London constituency, abolished in 1948, which was dominated by the votes of 'city men' who occupied business premises but did not reside there.

It may be argued on the other side that plural voting introduces extra administrative complications into the system; that it is not possible effectively to enforce rules that voters should vote (for instance) in not more than two constituencies; that it emphasises the anomalies involved in any system of special qualifications by awarding what looks like a scale of marks to electors according to their merit—and such a scale is bound to produce some absurd cases. But the attack is based mainly on the strong sentiment in favour of equal universal suffrage. 'One man one vote' is a very simple and appealing political cry: special qualifications of any kind are an obstacle in its way: to provide that special qualifications are to be cumulative adds a second obstacle which it is easy to denounce. The additional 'braking' effect of plural voting may be more apparent than real, as it offers new arguments to those pressing for change.

CHAPTER IV

Communal Representation

1. *Causes and consequences*

This is a subject of such political importance that it deserves a separate chapter, although its mechanics are implicit in what has already been said. The last chapter was written in terms of the rules for constituting a list of voters; but voters can act only within constituencies each returning one or several members. Such constituencies may be delimited on a territorial basis, or on some other basis, or on a mixture of bases. It is assumed nowadays that the normal practice is that of a single set of territorial constituencies; but we have seen that in Britain until 1948 there existed alongside the general territorial constituencies a set of non-territorial graduates' constituencies. A system of communal representation is one which gives first place to non-territorial considerations in forming constituencies: it links together voters from the whole country on the basis of characteristics other than that of attachment to a particular locality. The 'communal rolls' thus formed may be subdivided territorially for purposes of an election: but the 'communal' characteristic is given priority over the 'general' characteristic which everyone may possess, that of attachment to some locality.

The existence of University constituencies in Britain did not make the British system a 'communal' one, for two reasons. The first is that they occupied a very subordinate position in a system primarily territorial. In New Zealand 4 seats out of 80 are reserved for Maori candidates and voters, but the other seats are open to all candidates alike, those of mixed blood less than half Maori can register on the general roll, and the working of the system as a whole is little affected by the existence of 'reserved seats'. The second reason is that 'communalism' has become associated in ordinary discussion with the use of electoral qualifications based on race, language or religion in societies where these factors are of extreme political importance. It was at one time suggested quite seriously that British representation should be reorganised by extending enormously the system of graduates' constituencies, so that there would be separate constituencies (for instance) for doctors, teachers, and lawyers, for railwaymen, miners, dock workers, civil servants, engineering workers and so on. Such a system might replace the territorial system, or it might exist alongside it, either in the same House of Parliament or in a separate House. An arrangement on these lines would be

32

very difficult to reconcile with other principles of a system of 'free elections', and it has not in fact been tried for the principal assembly[1] except in Fascist countries, where a 'corporative' system of representation can be made to serve the ends of a particular kind of political management. But if it were tried it would be a system of 'pluralism', not of 'communalism': one could imagine a true case of 'communal' electorates within the United Kingdom if one supposed that in Northern Ireland Catholic voters and Protestant voters (who are about equal in numbers) were placed on separate rolls and voted in separate constituencies.

The extreme case of communal representation is that contained in the Government of India Act of 1935, which set India on its way towards self-government with no less than ten separate electorates for the Federal Assembly, apart from separate representation of a large number of Indian States. Perhaps no one at the time thought this a satisfactory or even a possible basis for Cabinet government in a free state: yet it seemed the best compromise available after long negotiation.

This hopeless position had been reached in two stages. Elections of the Western type were first introduced in India when self-government still seemed to be a long way off. The government's decision that communal elections should be commenced was not inspired by the wish to 'divide and rule'—though it might have served this end if Britain had in fact been anxious to hold India by force—but by the wish to follow the natural divisions of the country, and to consult such organised bodies of opinion as existed.[2] It was as natural for the British in India to consult Hindus and Muslims separately as it was for a medieval king to consult the 'estates' of his realm separately. All the earliest Western parliaments were formed in this way; in Sweden there survived until 1865 a Parliament consisting of the four 'estates' of Nobles, Clergy, Burghers, and Peasants. Once this first step had been taken in India, communal electorates grew stronger and proliferated with the approach of self-government. Each 'community' sought to protect itself by claiming a separate electorate, and by seeking to 'entrench' this in the constitution, in the hope that it might exercise some power in a free India by manipulating its votes in Parliament in combination with the votes of other minorities.

In India communalism is a matter of religion and community rather than of race and colour, but the political problem is not fundamentally different from that of countries which include a number of different

---

[1] The Irish Senate has some 'corporative' features, but its importance in Irish politics is limited.
[2] Similar 'communal' franchises were introduced by Persian nationalists in Persia in the Electoral Law which followed the revolution there in 1906. See Professor Ann K. S. Lambton: 'The Impact of the West in Persia'. *International Affairs*, Vol. 33, p. 20.

races. Much talk about the special difficulties of government in 'multi-racial' societies is coloured by presumptions about 'racial superiority' for which there is no ethical or scientific justification. But here too the underlying problem is one of community, of differences in creed and culture, in economic status and social organisation. Colour of skin may be a conspicuous badge of community: but 'communalism' without colour prejudice is an ancient way of life in very large areas of Africa, the Middle East and Asia, and exists wherever there are social groupings (as the Jewish community has been in Western Europe) which are widespread geographically yet coherent in culture and organised so as to give mutual aid independently of the machinery of the state. Communalism is compatible with a territorial state organisation so long as the state is above and outside the communities, and rules them by authority, consultation and compromise. But it is a matter of extreme difficulty to adapt to a communal society the system of free elections evolved in countries where (in spite of many internal divisions) the tradition of the nation is stronger than the tradition of communities within it. If the sentiment of national unity is strong, it may induce majorities to be tolerant towards minorities, minorities to accept without violent resistance the verdict of a majority vote. The emergence of nationalism, and of parties demanding national self-government, has made it important in a number of new states to reconcile communalism with majority voting in territorial constituencies; without the driving force of nationalism the reconciliation is impossible, even with its support the period of transition is likely to be an extremely delicate one.

During this period the use of communal rolls may be inevitable, because there is great pressure on the government to concede elections, and the state of society is such that it would not be realistic to elect representatives except as representatives of separate communities. If this path is chosen there are relatively few difficulties in the initial stages. The general administrative problems are much the same as with any other kind of constituency, and may be simplified because community organisations give help. There is a special technical problem of framing legislation to allocate each citizen to his own proper communal roll. It is not always easy to frame a legal definition of a 'Hindu' or an 'Anglo-Indian' or a 'European' or a 'Coloured Person'. But in a 'communal' society there are in practice few doubtful cases, and such as exist are politically unimportant. On the whole, each community knows its members, few are anxious to detach themselves from their own people and join with others. The technical difficulties are serious only where there is a fairly large indeterminate class (like the 'Coloured' people in South Africa) covering a wide variety of ways of life, so that they overlap other social groups.

Yet this is one of the few matters within the range of political science in which there is complete agreement between theory and practical experience. Communal elections strengthen communal feeling, because in public debate appeals are made principally to the interest of each community, and within each community the more violent and selfish spokesmen of special interests outbid the moderate and public-spirited. People entering public life learn first to talk the language of communal politics, not that of national politics; communalism may thus defeat nationalism, and destroy the possibility of national self-government.

2. *Mitigations*

It is easy therefore to advise governments interested in promoting independence under free elections to avoid at all costs the introduction of separate communal rolls, because a first false step can never be made good. But such advice is often Utopian; governments may have no choice, and the problem in practice may be to consider what can be done to reconcile communal sentiment (and even perhaps limited communal electorates) with majority rule. There is no satisfactory answer to this, but various devices have been tried or suggested.

(a) It was said above that the old British University constituencies were not numerous enough to create real 'pluralism' in the electoral system. Similarly, there is no true 'communalism' if all vote on a single common roll, and then in addition electors specifically qualified by belonging to a minority vote a second time on a separate roll of their own for a few seats in the legislature. The element of communalism is not important even if common roll and communal role are made mutually exclusive, so that the minority who vote on the latter are excluded from the former, so long as the communal roll controls only a small proportion of all the seats.

(b) Such an arrangement provides for minority representations, but it does not *guarantee* it. A law regulating the franchise is in most countries an ordinary law which can be altered by normal legislative procedure; a guarantee can be provided only by some kind of 'entrenched clause'. It can for example be provided in a formal constitution, subject to judicial enforcement by a court independent of the majority in the legislature, that laws affecting the franchise can be changed only by some special procedure. A two-thirds majority instead of a bare majority may be required in the legislature, or (if the legislature has two houses) in both houses sitting together. Or the constitution may provide for an 'Upper House' in which minorities are represented out of proportion to their numbers, so that they can block a bill which threatens their own position. This sort of 'entrenchment' is effective only if the entrenchment is itself entrenched; that is to say, if the constitution cannot itself be changed by some easier procedure so as to revise the clause giving protection to minorities. It was a flaw of this kind which in the end enabled the Afrikaner government in South Africa to repeal the entrenched clause protecting the position of coloured voters on the common roll in the Cape Province, in such a way that there was little risk of challenge by the courts (though as an extra precaution the majority also used its power to alter the composition of the relevant court).

Much ingenuity can be spent on such arrangements; but experience has been that 'entrenchment' is of little value when faced by the persistent hostility of a solid majority, which in the end brushes it aside either by ingenuity or by open breach of the constitution. Protective clauses are valuable only in marginal cases, where a number of separate interests are protected by the constitution, and a threat to one interest (which might be weak in isolation) creates an alliance of interests which have a common interest in defending the protection given them by the constitution. Such circumstances do arise—in federations, for instance —but outside them entrenchment is of little service except for a transitional period.

(c) It is often forgotten that even a system of territorial constituencies may ensure representation of minorities. This happens in its extreme form only when a large part of the minority community forms the majority in some parts of the country; it is obvious that there is no danger that Welshmen or miners will be unrepresented at Westminster, Middle Western Scandinavians, Boston Irish or Southern 'lily-whites' at Washington. The same thing may happen less obtrusively where there is a smaller concentration; then minority representation can be ensured by some kind of proportional voting, or the minority may be able to sell its votes to the party most willing to support its interests.

Minority spokesmen are therefore acutely interested in electoral geography. The situation may be such as to safeguard their interests without special interference; but in a marginal case the balance can be tipped one way or the other by 'fiddling' with constituency boundaries. The control of electoral 'districting' is a strategical point referred to in Chapter XII; its importance here is that if the power is used with ingenuity and benevolence it may be possible to frame constituencies in which minority representation is secure, as was done for the Tamil constituencies in Ceylon under the Donoughmore constitution of 1931.

(d) Finally, a word should be said of a device which was evolved as a compromise in the struggle between orthodox Hindus and 'scheduled castes' in the 1930's. The 'communal award' made by the British Prime Minister in the absence of agreement between the communities gave separate electorates to the Hindu 'untouchables', led by the late Dr. Ambedkar. Gandhi by one of his most famous fasts forced Dr.

Ambedkar to concede a system under which the scheduled castes should have not a separate electoral roll, but reserved seats on a common electoral roll. There were to be a number of constituencies in each of which one seat out of several would be reserved for a 'scheduled caste' member. The candidate or candidates for this seat would be chosen by the scheduled castes themselves in a sort of primary election; but in the main election they would vote along with orthodox Hindus on a common roll. Scheduled caste voters and orthodox Hindus would thus vote together for candidates of both 'shades'; the principle of common roll, and many of its political effects, would be preserved; but the scheduled castes would be sure of a specified number of seats filled by their own people.

Such a compromise may be complicated in operation, and is perhaps no more than a transitional device. But it still remains part of the electoral law of independent India; and a variant of it is to be tried in Tanganyika in the first elections to the legislature there in 1958.

CHAPTER V

The Candidates

1. *Introductory*

This chapter falls into three sections of unequal weight, dealing respectively with the qualifications of candidates, exclusion of frivolous candidates, and the nomination of candidates. The last section is by far the most important, because in all developed electoral systems members of the legislature and other elected holders of office are chosen through a process which involves two stages. Candidates generally have little chance of success unless supported by an effective party organisation; the situation is often that in practice each party chooses between its possible candidates, the electorate chooses between the parties, paying perhaps some attention to the personal merits of individual candidates, but moved primarily by the reputation and arguments of the parties. In extreme cases, where the party holds a completely 'safe seat', the first stage is the decisive one; nomination as candidate involves election, and in that constituency opposition votes can be regarded only as a gesture of dissent.

Such a situation may seem in some areas to be very like that of 'one-party democracy', or 'guided' elections. It differs from it so long as free opposition voting is allowed and there is a balance of parties in the country as a whole. There is a considerable area in the Southern States of the U.S.A. which returns only Democratic party representatives, so that the choice is in effect made by the party and not by the voters. In the United Kingdom at least a third of the members of the House of Commons are returned for 'safe seats', divided about equally between the two great parties. Both in America and in Britain the election as a whole is usually a close contest, keenly contested, and the electorate makes a real and decisive choice between parties. Nevertheless, party choice of candidates is so important as to cause considerable heart-searching about the question of democracy within the parties.

2. *Qualifications*

Lines of argument about qualifications for candidates follow closely those about qualifications for voters, and need not be discussed at great length. It may be held that any voter is good enough to be a candidate—and this generally follows if equal universal suffrage is conceded; or that candidates should in some way excel the ordinary

38

voter, by holding (for instance) higher property or educational qualifications. It is rare to find in practice the third possibility, that candidates need not themselves possess the qualifications of voters, but it is
not unknown. The second of them, that of special qualifications for
candidates, is much commoner, but it is hard to maintain once a wide
franchise has been conceded. Such provisions are easy to evade and do
very little to influence the choice of candidates at the vital point, that
of decision within the party.

There are, however, three minor matters which are sometimes important:

(a) *Locality rule.* Should a candidate be qualified as a voter in the constituency for which he stands? This would generally mean that he must
reside in his constituency; and sometimes such a 'locality rule' is
enforced by public opinion even though it has no legal basis. The
American Congress is the strongest instance of this, but it is not the only
one. Perhaps the arguments here differ according to whether executive
power is in the hands of a directly elected President or of a Cabinet
consisting primarily of elected members of the legislature. A President
backed by a national party and national public opinion may be able to
work well with a legislature consisting primarily of local people; but
such an assembly would not provide a very good national cabinet.
Cabinet government perhaps works best if based upon an assembly
which includes a sector of 'carpet-bagging' politicians, interested
primarily in national politics and ambitious for high office, and also a
sector of 'local worthies' who speak primarily for sectional interests.
If this is true, it is an argument against the introduction of a formal
locality rule in combination with responsible Cabinet government: but
it must be admitted that it is primarily a generalisation from the long
history of relations between the government and the House of Commons
in Britain.

(b) *Incompatibility of office.* British practice also established precedents
about incompatibility of office, and these empirical rules were later
generalised in the theory of separation of powers. This requires that
no member of the legislature should be at the same time an active
member of the judiciary or of the administration; the rule about the
administration admits of exceptions for 'high political office' in countries
under responsible Cabinet government. The strict doctrine of separation of powers is too rigid for daily use, but there is no doubt at all that
public confidence in the fairness of the electoral system cannot be
maintained unless some line is drawn between the roles of judge, civil
servant, and party politician. The line is sometimes shadowy, but if it
not drawn there is no chance of establishing the tacit understandings
which are necessary for the operation of free elections.

There may, however, be some doubt whether the holding of judicial or administrative office should be a disqualification for *candidature*, or only for *membership*. That is to say, may a judge or civil servant stand as candidate without resigning his post, and resign it only if he is elected? The most generous provision[1] of all is that in use in some European countries (such as Sweden and France[2]) that a civil servant if elected is suspended from his post in the administration, but need not abandon his pension rights and other privileges by resigning; if he loses his seat later, he may return to the Civil Service without loss of seniority. The decision here rests on a balance of considerations. On the one hand, any suggestion that the administration is 'playing politics' is dangerous to public confidence, and such risks can be taken safely only in countries like those of Scandinavia, where the tradition of free government is very old and stable. In France the connection between the higher Civil Service and party politics is close enough to cause some suspicion about the fairness of elections, especially in overseas territories. On the other hand, a rigid application of the rule that no servant of the government may present himself as a candidate (in its severest form the rule is that no such person may be a candidate until a considerable time—say two years—after resignation from the service) excludes a large number of able and experienced people from political life; this sacrifice may be a serious matter in a dependent territory where at first almost all who receive higher education enter into government service.

(c) *Refusal of seat.* It is fairly common for the candidate of a localised minority to fight and win an election, and then to protest against the basis of the state by refusing to take his seat, or by entering the House at its first sitting and provoking a row over the taking of the oath tendered to members. A state free enough to allow such incidents generally offers other means of protest which involve less waste of public money and time; it is not unreasonable to insist that candidates should at the time of nomination make a declaration that it is their intention to take their seats if elected, and to fulfil any necessary conditions about allegiance.

3. *Exclusion of frivolous candidates.*

Under some systems of voting candidates who have no serious chance of being elected may influence the poll adversely by splitting the vote

---

[1] Or almost the most generous: there is at least one example, that of the German 'Land' of Bavaria, where a civil servant may be an elected member and continue to act as a civil servant at the same time.

[2] In France, civil servants whose office gives them great influence in one locality may not be candidates while in office in that locality, or within six months of leaving it.

into fragments and so handing the seat to the best-organised minority. A well-known case is that of the elections in British Guiana in 1953 which led quickly to public disturbances and the suspension of the constitution. This danger is perhaps best met either by modifications in the voting system (Chapter VII, § 2), or by the natural growth of party organisation, or by both. If it is not met in any of these ways, there may be a case for some provision intended to discourage frivolous candidates from standing. Two forms of this are usual: to insist on a rather large number of signatures for a valid nomination, or to require a substantial deposit in cash from each candidate, to be forfeited by those who do not receive a stated percentage of the votes cast.

4. Primary elections and the recognition of parties

The procedure for nomination is in itself a simple matter, but careful regulation of formalities is required to prevent controversy about nominations alleged to be invalid. A 'drill' has to be laid down, providing for time and place of nomination, number of nominators, authentication of nominators, authentication of candidate's qualifications, payment of deposit (if required), making of any necessary declaration by the candidate. The details of this 'drill' are not important; all that is essential is that there should be strict procedure properly carried out.

Serious difficulties arise only when an attempt is made to enforce freedom in the choice of candidates by interfering in the affairs of parties so as to establish some open procedure for the choice of party nominees. Procedure of this kind was introduced first in the U.S.A., has been copied in Western Germany, but is rarely found elsewhere. The oldest American tradition is that party candidates for electoral office should be selected after voting at a 'convention' of party representatives; but a large assembly is not competent to discuss properly the merits of a long list of candidates, and the effect was in practice that conventions deliberated seriously only about nominations for a few very important offices, and then accepted without discussion the 'slate' of candidates for minor offices put forward by the 'platform' or party machine. Such offices though small in themselves may be important in a system of organised corruption; the saying of an eminent party boss has become proverbial, that he did not mind who won the election, so long as he could control the nominations on both sides.

At one time it was thought by reformers that the stranglehold of the bosses could be broken if party candidates were chosen not by a convention, but by the rank and file of the party, voting in what came to be called a 'primary election' to decide between all who wished to put their names forward as potential candidates. The expectations of reformers have on the whole been disappointed, since with a little extra effort a boss can influence a primary election about minor offices almost as easily as he can a convention; but their efforts have led to an unusually explicit recognition in the U.S.A. that election by a mass electorate is bound to involve two stages, and is therefore in a sense an indirect election. Primary elections are certainly of some value in a country with a free and energetic press, since they bring the internal problems of the parties before the public, and submit the parties to pressure by public opinion. A dissident member of a party has the opportunity to appeal from the bosses to the rank and file; such revolts do not succeed very often, but they always attract public attention, and the threat of serious trouble at the primaries is of some importance in shaping the behaviour of American parties and party managers.

It would be out of place to attempt to explain here the enormous complications of the American system of primaries, which are a matter for the states and not for the federal government, and are therefore regulated by 48 different sets of laws.[1] But something must be said of even wider issues about the legal recognition and regulation of political parties. Parties play an integral part in elections because they are in effect the nominators of candidates, and they also intervene in many other ways, some of which will appear in later chapters. It is no infringement of freedom that the state should regulate in some respects the activities of bodies which intervene directly in a vital part of the operation of the state. Indeed, part of the case for the regulation of parties is that it cuts through the illusion that the great parties of modern states can be regarded simply as private associations. The case against it rests not on principle but on the difficulties of application.

In its simplest form such regulation proceeds, by argument from the assumption that all effective candidates have party backing, to exclude candidates who have no party backing, and are therefore superfluous. This raises two questions. What parties are to be recognised? What constitutes 'party backing'?

(a) The answer to the first question is important for list systems of proportional representation (below, Chapter IX) as well as for the nomination of candidates under any form of voting procedure. The question divides naturally into two further questions: is the party a substantial one? does it propose to work within the constitution, not to subvert it?

A niggardly answer to the former question can be given by requiring that a party shall not be recognised in a constituency unless it obtained $x\%$ of the total votes cast in that constituency (or in the whole country) at the last election (that is to say, new parties, or parties formed by sub-division, are excluded); or it may be answered liberally—and in a

---

[1] A convenient account of the main problems is to be found in V.O. Key: *Politics, Parties and Pressure Groups* (New York, 1952), Ch. 14.

way that invites faking—by a requirement that a new party should be backed by a petition signed by x% of the registered voters, or that it should put up candidates in x% of the constituencies (the latter is the formula used by the B.B.C. in deciding on the time to be allocated to each party for political broadcasts). Convenience and justice can best be served by a combination of the two systems.

The question about the purpose of a party can be answered in a strict way only by requiring a formal statement of the party's objects and ideology. Very few parties with long traditions can do this in a coherent way: imagine a legally drafted statement of the objects of the British Conservatives, or the American Democrats, or the French Radical Socialists! But if no strict statement of purpose is required from them, parties can be excluded as subversive only if considerable discretion is entrusted to some authority, either judical or administrative; a power invidious to exercise and dangerous to political freedom.

(b) Regulation on these lines results in the creation of legal entities called 'political parties' which are entitled to contest elections by proposing candidates. It is almost inevitable that the law creating such a legal entity should also recognise within it a governing body which if properly constituted may legally give the party's official consent. In its simplest form, a law requiring that all candidates should have party backing may stipulate only that the party should signify assent through the signature of its secretary, or by appending its official seal, or in some other formal way. But this is not very satisfactory to those interested in freedom of candidature, because it leaves the ultimate choice of elected persons in the hands of the unspecified 'bosses' of the various approved parties. Hence the doctrine of primary elections, which follows logically from the principle of legal recognition of parties, but involves also an attempt at state regulation of democracy within parties, an attempt which has never been conspicuously successful.

The dilemma can be explained by three examples, of necessity much simplified. In Britain no legal recognition whatever is given to the part played by parties in elections; this is admirably simple, but there is no doubt that the process of selecting candidates is one of the less open and admirable parts of British democracy. In the U.S.A. there are many different forms of regulation, but it might be fair to generalise by saying that the attempt to regulate parties by introducing primary elections has introduced complications quite unintelligible to the ordinary elector, and therefore not successful in reassuring him about his freedom of choice. In some European countries the regulation of parties, introduced in theory to protect the state and the electors, has become in practice a matter of mutual support between existing parties, which disagree about many things but unite to protect their common interest by excluding new parties. Under such a system, elections may be genuinely free, in that the elector has quite a wide range of choice between parties; but the choice between candidates within each party is exercised solely by the local or national party machines.

All these systems work with a reasonable degree of freedom, none is perfectly satisfactory. If elections are to be introduced in new settings, a decision must be made quite early about what is to be done regarding the legal position of parties, and a decision once taken tends to perpetuate itself. One course of action is to disregard parties and to require only the names of individuals as nominators of candidates; this avoids administrative problems, and allows political forces to make their way freely, but it may at first give extra power to organised minorities, and may later leave important decisions in the hands of party machines which have established themselves during the first phase. The alternative is to insist almost from the first that all candidates must be backed by a legally recognised party; this gives recognition from the outset to the essential place of parties in an electoral system, and helps their growth, but it throws an invidious burden on the administration and may tend to concentrate power in the hands of a small group of party leaders.

Part Two: Methods of Voting

CHAPTER VI

Indirect Elections

We have seen in the previous chapter that all elections with large electorates are in a sense indirect elections, because they depend to some extent on pre-selection of candidates by party organisations. There is nevertheless a great difference between this sort of operation and the idea of a pyramid of elections, in which the ordinary voter is at the base of the pyramid and the final choice of representatives is made by exalted persons several degrees above him. Under direct elections with a party system the candidates are chosen by relatively small groups of party members and party managers, but they are then submitted to the electorate as a whole; the final decision rests with the mass electorate, and there is in principle a direct relation between the voters and those who are elected. Under the other system the ordinary voter chooses merely someone to vote on his behalf; this 'voting agent' may then meet with other 'agents' to choose the delegate of this group to vote in the second stage of the election; and the final choice may be made by a relatively small group, meeting privately and acting at two removes from those whom they are deemed to represent. There is no doubt which system is preferable, if one of the main objects of free elections is to promote a sense of general consent to and participation in the process of government.

In spite of this, indirect elections may be a necessary step in preparing the way for direct elections in countries where the range of mass communications is at present very small. The illiterate tribesmen in the backward areas of the Sudan or of the Northern Region of Nigeria[1] perhaps understand little of what is involved when there is a village meeting to choose members of an electoral college one stage higher; but such meetings at least begin the process of awakening a sense that there can be national as well as local politics, and the effects may be rapid and lasting if with the development of indirect elections goes the spread of literacy, of radio sets and of well-staged party propaganda. Indirect elections in such an environment have perhaps more to do with political education than with political power; electoral colleges (such as those which elect French Senators) are notoriously a breeding-ground of personal intrigue, and their use in elections to an assembly may lead to government by cliques, which has few of the advantages of govern-

[1] The Northern Region now (1957) has direct elections.

ment by parties. Nevertheless, they may serve their turn in a period of transition.

The organisation of indirect elections depends largely on local factors, and the closest parallel is naturally that of local government elections. The procedure for voting at the base of the pyramid can take any of the forms described in the next chapters, and there are perhaps only two special points of some general importance:—

(a) The pyramid may 'build up' either to a series of colleges electing one member each; or to a series of colleges electing several members each; or to one large college electing together all the representatives who are to be chosen. The second two systems can scarcely be worked fairly without some form of proportional representation, and there are few objections to the single transferable vote system (Chapter VIII) when the electors are comparatively few in number and have the opportunity to meet for formal or informal discussion. It is obvious that each of the three systems may have rather different effects on the choice of members in a given geographical and social situation, and this flexibility is both an advantage and a disadvantage of indirect elections during a period of transition. The system is relatively easy to 'manage' so as to produce a result biased one way or another, and creates suspicions of 'management' even when these are not justified.

(b) A choice has also to be made between the use as electoral colleges of bodies elected for other purposes—usually as local authorities—and the creation of a separate pyramid of colleges concerned with nothing but central elections. Perhaps the most famous example of the former is its use for the Senate of the Third Republic in France, and for the Conseil de la République of the Fourth Republic: the latter method was used for the election of the Third Estate of the States General, which set going the French Revolution in 1789, and in other French constitutions of that period. It is objected, on the one hand, that the use of local authorities drags local government into national politics, and this adds to influences tending towards corruption in local government; on the other hand, that separate electoral colleges are not truly representative because those chosen are not those on whom simple voters really rely in their ordinary local business. Perhaps a system of separate colleges, energetically used, may be more successful than the other system in making educational propaganda for the idea of national elections: but it is rather unlikely that the use of local authorities has much effect in making them political—they are bound to become 'political' in any case, if the time is one of real political excitement.

The example of the French Senate suggests a final point. In the long run, there can be no public confidence in indirect elections as a method of choosing the main legislative assembly, but there is much to be said for them as a way of electing a second chamber, if it is decided that it is desirable to have one. A second chamber which is largely hereditary or nominated is likely to be ineffectual except as a body of technical experts, and there are other and better ways of obtaining specialist advice; a second chamber elected directly by the same suffrage as is used for the other house is likely to duplicate its opinions, unless (as in the Australian and American Senates) it has a federal basis giving a different balance of popular representation. If the object is to find in a unitary state a second chamber which has some power to check, and not merely to advise, the first chamber, it is perhaps best to seek it through indirect elections based on the membership of local authorities. This is the practice of Holland and Sweden as well as of France, and it has various advantages. Even in a state dominated by parties the members of local authorities are generally people of a different type from those who make a career of politics at the centre; a body elected by them rests on the support of local sentiments which are important to most electors and cannot readily be expressed in direct elections to the other house; and the composition of the electorate for the second chamber can be judiciously managed so as to give additional weight to those in whose interest the 'check' has been created—for instance, to the countryside against the towns, or to minorities against a solid block of votes held by the largest community.

CHAPTER VII

The 'First past the post' system
and its Variants

1. *Simple Plurality*

Electoral democracy rests on general acceptance of the convention that it is right and convenient in certain circumstances to take the formally expressed opinion of a part for the opinion of the whole, and that all are then bound in law and conscience by the decision taken. Such a convention is always found in democracies of this type, indeed it constitutes their special character or definition; but the practical bearing of the rule, like that of many such rules, depends on interpretation. What part is it of which the opinion is to prevail?

So far as concerns elections, the simplest and perhaps most naïve answer is to say that the candidate who gets the most votes is to win. This at least was the traditional English practice from the thirteenth century onwards, in electing 'two knights from every shire and two burgesses from every borough'; it was used at first in two-member constituencies (each elector having two votes), it was adopted in the nineteenth century for use in the now universal single-member constituencies, and it is by far the commonest form of voting in the 'Anglo-Saxon' countries. Outside them it is rare, because the system is justified by history rather than by logic. The traditional English practice of elections, from the sixteenth century to the early nineteenth century, was that seats were for the most part held solidly by a single local 'interest' or by an alliance of interests, and the process of electing two members was usually achieved by arrangement behind the scenes, without public contest. Occasionally such arrangements broke down, and there was then a contest in which interests were ranged against interests, swaying voters by all means at their command, legal and illegal. Until the 1830s electoral excitement in England arose not out of general elections involving the whole country, but out of jousts between individual champions in such constituencies as Middlesex, Westminster and Yorkshire. These rare events were expensive and often violent: they were certainly important to English liberties, but no one took them very seriously as expressions of 'the people's will' on matters of national policy. In these circumstances the 'first past the post' system, or to give it a more formal name, the 'simple plurality system', served as well as any other; it gave a fair

50

chance for tactical manoeuvring and alliances between individuals and interests, in an age when centralised parties did not exist. A result of this form would then be accepted by all as fair and decisive.

$$(1) \begin{cases} \star A & 900 \\ \star B & 750 \end{cases}$$
$$ \quad C \quad\quad 625$$
$$ \quad D \quad\quad 600$$

The old system of voting was not therefore the subject of much discussion at the time of the first Reform Act in Britain, that of 1832, and it survived unchanged in quite different political conditions. As the 19th century advanced, contests began to turn more on issues of public policy than on those of personal advancement. At the same time, the parties gradually grew stronger, until a general election assumed the aspect of a battle between opposing armies, and each party felt bound to incur the expense of contests even in hopeless seats. These developments transformed the working of the system, and exposed it to criticism on two main grounds.

First, the 'first past the post' system may have very odd results in a single-member constituency if all national parties feel bound to contest the seat, and some 'free-lances' join in. One can imagine an extreme case of the following pattern, though such absurdities are rare in practice:—

$\star$A	(Conservative)	12,000
B	(Labour)	11,000
C	(Liberal)	9,000
D	(Communist)	2,500
E	(Welsh Nationalist)	2,000
F	(Independent)	500
		37,000

Such a result would at once raise questions about the 'reality' or representation; does the winner 'really' represent the seat? Or has he merely been lucky? The position was perhaps somewhat better so long as two-member constituencies existed, since they offered some chance of bargaining between parties. But the last of these was abolished in 1948, and even two-member constituencies could give odd results in a period of strict party alignment. Here, for instance, is a real example (Stockport, 1945):

---

[1] '$\star$' here and later in these examples means 'elected'.

*Conservative	31,039
*Conservative	30,792
Labour	29,674
Labour	29,630
Liberal	14,994
Liberal	14,942

Secondly, if there are more than two parties of national importance a general election conducted on these lines may produce results that seem peculiar. A British election is now treated rather as a plebiscite between alternative governments than as a series of contests between individual candidates: it is customary to reckon up the total votes cast for each party in the country; and there are often very large variations in the relation between votes cast and seats gained. In 1924 each seat won cost the Conservatives 19,200 votes, the Labour Party 36,500 votes; in 1929 the figures were 33,400, and 29,210; in 1931, 22,900 and 127,000. In 1945 the Labour Party had a majority of 393 seats to 247, over all other parties in the House of Commons; but only 11,992,292 votes had been cast for it, 12,981,006 against. In 1955 the Conservatives had 345 seats against 285, 13,311,938 votes against 13,488,723 for all other parties. Results of this sort are dangerous because they cast some doubt on the government's title to rule, and may suggest that the system of election is merely a gamble.

There are various answers to these complaints. One of them is that the 'first past the post' system can only produce a representative elected by a minority in constituencies in which there are three or more parties in the field, and that it operates so as to redress this situation, if it occurs, by pressing hard upon the third party, cutting its representation below its votes until it decides to abandon the electoral struggle. The 'first past the post' system therefore tends to establish a two-party system (though there have been few periods in British history when this result has been completely attained); and this, it would be maintained on other grounds, is the best sort of party system.

Another answer is contained in mathematical researches which seem to have shown that so long as two parties between them obtain more than about 90% of the total votes cast there is bound to be a regular distribution of seats between them, not in proportion to votes cast but in proportion to the cube of votes cast. This is the famous 'cube law', the details of which are not here important; there is no doubt that, if allowance is made for certain other oddities in the system, the cube law is of value in deducing the composition of a future House of Commons from predictions about the division of the total votes between the main parties. The British system (it is said) is not a gamble, but an instrument for magnifying small majorities of voters so that they become large majorities in the House of Commons; and this (it would be maintained) is in itself a good thing.

Thirdly, there is the reply by way of counter-attack. The next two chapters deal with attempts to ensure that there is much greater proportionality between votes cast and seats won than is usual under the British system, and some at least of these systems are certainly better designed to reflect divisions of opinion among the electorate. To this it is retorted that the object of an election is not to take a snap-shot or offer a mirror image, but to obtain a decision. If the main object of elections were to reflect opinion, this could be better achieved by some system of selection of members by random sampling, or by a 'Gallup poll' of public opinion. What elections should do is to face the elector with a choice, which he is to make in a particular set of circumstances between alternatives which are real and present; responsibility must be thrust upon the electorate for facing real issues, making the best of available alternatives, and abiding by the decision taken. This can only be achieved completely (it is said) by 'straight' voting in single-member constituencies.

A balanced view might be that elections ideally require both a responsible electorate and a house fairly representative of its opinions; and that ingenuity in devising systems should be directed towards finding a compromise. There has been no lack of ingenuity; indeed, an excess of it has produced so many alternatives, of such complexity, that a new argument emerges for the old 'first past the post' system, the argument that it is less likely than any other system to be deliberately distorted by ingenious tacticians in the interest of one party or another. In the rest of this chapter we deal with variants of the 'first past the post' system which do not introduce anything that can properly be called proportional representation.

These can be divided, a little arbitrarily, into two groups: systems designed to ensure that no one is returned except by a majority (50% + 1) of those voting in the constituency; and those designed to ensure that minorities gain at least some representation. To achieve the latter requires multi-member constituencies, except in so far as minorities can be helped by ingenuity in tracing the boundaries of single-member constituencies.

2. Majority representation

The first group of variants rests on the assumption that 'the part whose opinion is to prevail' must be at least a majority. In elections this almost always means a majority of those actually voting, not a majority of those entitled to vote. An attempt may be made to deal with the problem of non-voters by introducing compulsory voting (below, Chapter XV, § 1(b)); there are sometimes constitutional provisions which require an assembly to take certain 'entrenched' decisions by a majority of its whole membership; but it would be impracticable in mass elections to give a block of voters the right to stop proceedings by abstention, which might prevent any decision from receiving the support of a majority of those entitled to vote.

(a) *Repeated ballots*. The simplest method is that sometimes used for elections made by assemblies: for instance, the election of candidates for the offices of President and Vice-President by an American party convention, of the President of the French Republic by a body composed of the National Assembly and the Council of the Republic voting together. Voting goes on through a series of ballots until some candidate obtains an absolute majority of the votes cast. In such a system the act of voting becomes an integral part of a process of political bargaining and compromise. At first, there are many candidates, some of whom are put forward only to establish a bargaining position or to satisfy some point of prestige. After each ballot there are negotiations behind the scenes about the withdrawal of hopeless candidates in favour of those who have a chance of success, and support is sold for what it is worth in terms of personal or political favours. The field is narrowed gradually until only three or four candidates remain, and voting may continue between them during a series of 'deadlocked' ballots. In the end, something cracks, and it becomes obvious who will win. At that stage, there is usually to be observed the famous 'band-wagon effect' of American nominating conventions; doubters rush to make their peace with the victor, and in the end someone (often not the leader on the first ballot) is returned with a clear majority, sometimes even with the cry 'let's make it unanimous'.

(b) *The second ballot*. Such a process smells of political intrigue, of the 'smoke-filled hotel bedrooms' in which party nominees for the American presidency are traditionally chosen. Nevertheless, it is a careful and realistic way of eliciting the political opinions of the voters, their opinions about practical politics, not about abstract theory. Clearly it cannot be adopted as it stands for use in mass elections[1], but there is a half-way house, the second ballot system, which was the characteristic system of elections under the Third Republic in France. A first ballot is held at which a candidate cannot be elected unless he obtains an absolute majority of the votes cast. The first ballot (if it does not return a member) gives a measure of strength for all the candidates, and there is a period of bargaining about withdrawals. Then (in France, after an interval of a week or a fortnight) there is a second ballot in the

[1] An exception is its use in open elections at village level in non-literate societies, where the whole electorate can meet in public and line up behind the candidates, proceeding through successive 'ballots' till one 'line' has the majority.

constituencies which require one, and this time the election goes by 'simple plurality' to the leading candidate.

This naturally reduces the number of seats held on a minority vote, a number which might be large in a country like France, where there are several well-established parties and the evolution of a two-party system is not generally thought to be desirable, because it might mean not party balance (as in Britain or the U.S.A.) but civil war. This reduction of minority successes is satisfactory in principle; and the second ballot has the further advantage that the bargaining process gives an opportunity for compromise among the less extreme parties. The Third Republic kept its balance, in spite of many storms, as a result of such 'transactions' between the parties and interests near the centre of the political spectrum, which had a common interest in stability. On the other hand, the spectacle of such bargaining is not morally attractive, and it tends to strengthen local interests against the centre, because no party headquarters can deal adequately with the tactical situation in each of five or six hundred constituencies. Hence the tendency in France to seek refuge from this system of *ballotage* in some form of proportional representation: but experiments in reform have generally been followed by a return to the old system. This is still a political possibility in the Fourth Republic.

(c) *The alternative vote.* The system of repeated balloting can be imitated by the use of ballot papers which enable the elector to indicate his order of preference by putting numbers opposite the names of candidates. Thus:—

Candidate	Vote
A	–
B	2
C	4
D	1
E	3

These numbers are instructions as to what to do with the elector's vote in certain circumstances. This is a single-member constituency, and the election is to be by an absolute majority. First preferences are counted first: suppose that at the first count the figures are:—

First Count	A	7,000
	C	5,500
	E	4,000
	B	2,500
	D	1,000
		20,000

D is assumed to have no chance and is eliminated; those who voted for him are 'asked' for whom they now wish to vote, by counting their second preferences. In the sample ballot paper above, the second preference was for B. At this second stage, the result might be:—

Second Count	A	7,250	(+250)
	C	6,000	(+500)
	E	4,150	(+150)
	B	2,600	(+100)

B is now eliminated, and the next preferences in his ballot papers are counted. (These may be either the second preferences of his original 2500 voters, or the third preferences of those—like our example—who voted first for D, second for B). The result must still be a deadlock, since C and E together have more than half the votes cast: let us picture two more stages:—

Third Count	A	8,250	(+1,000)
	C	6,900	(+ 900)
	E	4,850	(+ 700)

Fourth Count	★ C	10,750	(+3,850)
	A	9,250	(+1,000)

C is therefore elected on the fourth count, by votes which include the fourth preference of our imaginary voter, who preferred successively D, B and E.

The example is an extreme case in this respect, and also in that it assumes that all voters expressed preferences—this is not essential to the validity of a vote, and if he had understood this (as many do not) perhaps our voter would have preferred to 'abstain on the fourth ballot', by not expressing a fourth preference at all. But it serves to illustrate both the strength and the weakness of the system. Even in a tangled situation like that suggested by the example, it does elicit a majority view, on a basis somewhat like that of continued balloting within an assembly. But it is one thing to vote again and again, with time for reflection and discussion about each new situation as it arises; another thing to express by writing numbers on a piece of paper a hypothetical decision about a choice which cannot be foreseen exactly. One is left wondering whether our voter really would have preferred C to A, if he had been faced with a direct choice in a final 'run-off'.

In practice, these lower preferences can only be used effectively by voters who follow general directions from party headquarters, issued on the basis of bargaining between parties, and the alternative vote may therefore have an important effect on the results if there exist parties strong enough to bind their voters to a bargain. In 1930 a minority Labour government in Great Britain obtained temporary Liberal support in exchange for an undertaking to introduce a bill for the alternative vote. The Liberal Party was then in great danger of being squeezed out of existence between the two major parties: but if the alternative vote had been introduced it might have gained second preference votes from both sides in three-cornered fights, and it might also have strengthened its position by bargains, local or national, with one of the other parties for mutual support by the exchange of second preference votes. The proposal was swept away, by the crisis of 1931, a new split in the Liberal Party, and a disastrous general election, and it is now unlikely to be adopted in Britain.[1] It is, however, used in some Federal and State elections in Australia.

3. Minority representation

Under a system of simple plurality voting, whether in single-member or in multi-member constituencies, it is possible for a bare majority, or even for a minority, to take all the seats, if it is well organised and geographically well distributed. Probably the danger is greatest in small countries, such as British Guiana, where in the elections of 1953 a party, the P.P.P., which secured only 51% of the votes cast (and the poll was low) won three-quarters of the seats. But simple plurality voting almost always tells in favour of the biggest organised groups against smaller ones. There are various ways of counteracting this tendency without having recourse to proportional representation, but they all require the use of multi-member constituencies.

(a) *The single non-transferable vote.* The simplest scheme is to give each elector one vote only in a multi-member constituency. Suppose a constituency in which 7,000 electors actually vote, which is to elect

---

[1] It was used between 1918 and 1949 in the single-member University constituencies, London, Wales, and Belfast.

six members; each elector has one vote only, and any candidate supported by 1,001 voters is bound to be elected. This is obviously true, because out of 7,000 votes not more than six candidates can possibly obtain 1,001 votes $(7,000 - (1,001 \times 6) = 994)$. The formula by which this figure is reached is $\left(\dfrac{\text{votes cast}}{\text{(seats to be filled} + 1)} + 1 \right)$, and is known after the name of its discoverer as the Droop quota: it will be necessary to refer to this again later, as it is important in systems of proportional representation.

In practice, with a single *non*-transferable vote, a candidate who gets less than the Droop quota may be elected: for instance:—

A	1,300 ★
B	1,150 ★
C	1,050 ★
D	1,000 ★
E	800 ★
F	700 ★
G	600
Others together	400
	——
	7,000

Indeed this is the most probable pattern of voting: all the system ensures is that any body of voters capable of organising themselves effectively behind the right number of candidates—not too many, not too few—is likely to be successful more or less in proportion to its numbers. The system gives a much larger bonus to good organisation than does the single *transferable* vote, described in the next chapter.

The single non-transferable vote has been used in elections in Japan since 1900, but there has been so little study of these elections that it would be unwise to draw conclusions from them.

(b) *The limited vote* is an application of the same principle and was used in England for a short period after the Reform Act of 1867, which created a number of three-member constituencies in large towns. To reduce the preponderance of the majority party, each elector was given only two votes for three seats. Suppose a city in which there were on the register 27,000 Conservatives and 20,000 Liberals: under the simple plurality system the Conservatives would have three votes each, and if they put up three candidates and no more, and voted solid, they were bound to carry all three seats. But if they had only two votes each, 54,000 votes in all, they could not give more than 18,000 votes to each of three Conservative candidates, whereas the Liberals if they put up only one candidate could give him 20,000 votes and elect him. What is more, the Liberals would then still have a second vote to give to the Conservative whom they liked best, or disliked least, and they might well get him in. The Conservatives could stop this Liberal intervention in their affairs by putting up only two candidates; the Liberals could wreck their own chances by putting up a second Liberal candidate. The practical effect of the system was therefore to induce bargains between the parties to divide the representation, and to discourage 'wild-cat' candidates who might split the party vote. It also encouraged party discipline by giving a great advantage to a party whose voters were prepared to follow instructions. Suppose that in this case the figure was 33,000 Conservatives, not 27,000. By judicious instructions about the divisions of 66,000 votes between three candidates, the Conservatives could ensure that each of the three got about 22,000 votes, as against a Liberal maximum of 20,000, and if discipline prevailed they could thus carry all the seats.

(c) *The cumulative vote.* A somewhat similar result is obtained if each voter is given as many votes as there are seats in a multi-member constituency, and is allowed to divide them as he pleases, perhaps giving them all to one candidate. This was the system used in the elections to School Boards in Great Britain from 1870 to 1902, a period when it was important to ensure that reasonable representation was given to religious minorities in the control of local education. Suppose a Board of seven members, elected by a single constituency in which 8,000 electors vote, each of them having seven votes. 56,000 votes are cast, 7 members are to be elected; the Droop formula shows that anyone who secures 7001 votes is certain to be elected. The result is in fact much the same as that of the single non-transferable vote, but the voter (and the party managers who advise him) is given rather more freedom of choice, because he can either concentrate his votes on one candidate or distribute them among several.

(d) *Points systems and fractional systems.* It is possible to carry the same principle further, by inventing devices which in effect give the voter *more* votes than there are seats to be filled, and enable him (within limits defined in each system) to put candidates in order of preference by the way in which he divides votes between them. In the example of the cumulative vote given above, a voter with seven votes could indicate a preference by distributing them between three candidates, in the ratio four, two, one. If he were given twenty-one votes, obviously he could indicate a wider range of choice with greater subtlety of discrimination: and the position is exactly the same if he is given one vote and is allowed to divide it into fractions. Or he can be instructed simply to mark candidates in order of preference on the ballot-paper, and his ordinal numbers will be translated by prescribed rules into cardinal numbers, or points, or fractions, and these points or fractions will be added together to give each candidate his total.

It is hard to see what is gained by these refinements, and Miss Lakeman and Mr. Lambert in their comprehensive book on voting systems cite only one example of their use in practice. All minority safeguards of this type work in the same direction, to protect the representation of minority interests capable of disciplined organisation. The more complicated the system, the greater the premium offered to good organisation.

CHAPTER VIII

The Single Transferable Vote

1. *Introductory*

A system of proportional representation may be defined as a system of voting which includes some device for allocating seats proportionately to the votes cast for each candidate (or affiliated group of candidates) in the constituency concerned. This definition suggests some preliminary observations:—

(a) P.R. (the abbreviation will be used for brevity hereafter) requires multi-member constituencies; one seat cannot be divided proportionately.

(b) The larger the number of seats in the constituency the more exact is the proportionality that can be achieved.[1] The element of proportionality that can be achieved in allocating two seats is trivial (though an attempt was made in some of the old University constituencies in England), it begins to be significant in a three-member constituency, reaches the maximum possible only if the whole country is treated as a single constituency, electing the whole assembly together. Advocates of P.R. generally suggest that valuable results can be obtained by one or other form of the system in constituencies of from five to seven members.

(c) None of the systems described in Chapter VII comes within this definition of P.R. The modifications of 'first past the post' which are there described are designed either to ensure that no one is elected unless he secures a majority, or that substantial and well-organised minorities secure some representation. Such devices may make the system more acceptable; they may in doing so increase its proportionality; but this improvement in proportionality is secured incidentally, and not by direct contrivance. There is a difference, subtle but important, between systems which aim at something else and incidentally increase proportionality, and those which make proportionality their purpose (or one of their purposes) and therefore have some proportional device 'built into' them.

(d) There are two main types of P.R., described in this chapter and the next, the 'single transferable vote' and the 'list system'. Each has many variants, and it is possible to combine them with one another, or even to mix them ingeniously with the 'first past the post' system.

[1] This is shown very neatly in a graph by Miss Enid Lakeman and J. D. Lambert (*Voting in Democracies*, p. 115).

Some of these special 'prescriptions' will be described in Chapter X, and reference will be made to the issues of principle which they raise. The first step, however, is to explain the S.T.V. system and the list system in their pure forms.

2. S.T.V.: Origins and formula

It is important to realise that the S.T.V. system was invented before the growth of modern party organisation in Europe. In the 1830s and 1840s there was growing acceptance of the thesis of de Tocqueville's famous book *Democracy in America*, the first part of which was published in 1835, that democracy in the sense of government based on direct universal suffrage was certain to come in Western Europe within a relatively short time. De Tocqueville held up to Europe the mirror of America, and Europe saw there the grave danger (as it was believed to be) that universal suffrage would lead to the 'tyranny of the majority'. He thought that this tyranny was manifest in the developed party system of the U.S.A., which set two or three great organisations in competition for votes, and offered large prizes to the party which secured the majority: and he held this form of politics responsible for the form of American society, which seemed to French intellectuals (as it seemed to English middle-class writers like Mrs. Trollope and Charles Dickens) to be vulgar, conformist, and mediocre, in spite of its great energy. In the U.S.A. (it was recognised) the effects of majority rule were to some extent mitigated by the distribution of power within the federal system; but these checks created other problems and indeed led eventually to the civil war of 1861. In Europe the demand in Germany and Italy, and even in the Hapsburg monarchy, was for consolidation, not federalism, and popular sovereignty could not be limited in that way. Something might be done with ingeniously constructed second chambers, but the crux of the matter lay in finding an electoral system which conceded the demand for universal suffrage, and so halted the irresistible pressure on which that demand was based, but did not in the process give all power to party leaders controlling the votes of the majority. Such parties did not then exist outside the U.S.A., and there were not therefore vested interests to be provided for in constructing an electoral system. The aim of constitutional theorists was to strengthen the position of the individual candidate, and to encourage loosely organised minorities, so as to secure an assembly of intelligent and capable men, representing opinion in the country, but not dominated by party machines.

The S.T.V. system in its developed form is undoubtedly the best answer to this problem. The question now is not whether it is a good device, but whether this is a real problem. Cruder devices for the same purpose, such as the second ballot, the limited vote and the cumulative vote, had been invented earlier, and apparently S.T.V. was devised independently at about the same time in the 1850s by a liberal Danish politician, C. C. G. Andrae, and by a London barrister, Thomas Hare, whose view of politics was also progressive but not radical. The system achieved fame because it was seized upon by John Stuart Mill, the intellectual leader of British liberalism, and was built into the structure of his book on *Representative Government*, published in 1861. His book was for two generations the text-book of British liberal constitution-makers, and remains the best statement of their point of view. There have been refinements in the methods of S.T.V., but little has been added to the arguments about principle contained in Chapter VII of Mill's book and in the answer to them in Chapter V of Walter Bagehot's book on *The English Constitution*, published in 1867.

The principle of the S.T.V. system is that there should be multi-member constituencies in which each voter has only one vote, however numerous the seats to be filled. The voter is to cast that vote for the individual whom he or she (the voter) most wishes to have as representative, and is to have the greatest possible chance to make his vote 'effective' by casting it for someone actually elected. The 'model' is that of repeated ballots in a multi-member constituency in which each voter has one vote only.

Suppose a five-member constituency in which there are 6,000 voters casting between them 6,000 votes. On the principle of the Droop quota, explained on p. 58, any candidate securing 1,001 votes must be elected. Suppose then that voters vote individually by a system which records each vote as it is cast: as soon as a candidate obtains 1,001 valid votes, he is declared elected. No more votes can be cast for him, and the election proceeds among the other candidates. Suppose that by the time all electors have voted once, only three candidates have obtained 1,001 votes; there are seven candidates dividing between them the other 2,997 votes, and in the end (of course) only two of them can get as many as 1,001 votes. We proceed next either by asking for withdrawals or by disqualifying the candidate who had the smallest vote on the first round: in either case the voters who have not yet voted for a successful candidate are asked to choose among the surviving candidates—they are not *compelled* to vote for one of them, but may do so if they please. This is the 'second round': the process can be repeated in third and later rounds of voting if necessary. The result will in the end be that in an electorate of 6,000 any individual who commands the support of 1,001 voters will certainly be returned; only 1,000 voters at the most, out of 6,000, will have voted for someone who did not need their vote or for someone who failed to be elected; and if the voters are divided in their voting by party, nationality, religion, class, or other factors, the allocation of seats will be roughly proportional to those divisions between the voters. It will be *exactly* proportional to the division of votes, *excluding* (at most) voters fewer by one than the Droop quota. As the number of seats increases, the Droop quota becomes relatively smaller.

A system of this kind (which is virtually never used in practice) would be analogous to the system of repeated ballots in a single-member constituency (explained on p. 54), which cannot of course secure proportionality. The S.T.V. system bears the same relation to the alternative vote system: it is an attempt to carry out the whole of such a series of ballots together, by asking each voter to give an indication of preference on his ballot paper. For purposes of illustration, it is enough to postulate a three-member constituency with seven candidates: but it is to be remembered that advocates of the system recommend the use of rather larger constituencies in order to secure a higher degree of proportionality. We shall imagine a situation not unlike the present position in British party politics, but perhaps made somewhat less rigid by the introduction of S.T.V. There are three Conservative candidates; one of them (B) is a very well-known national figure, the other two (C and G) are not much respected local men, who are in effect competing against one another for a seat, because no one believes that in this constituency the Conservatives can win all three seats, although they may win two of them. Labour has two candidates (A and F) one of whom (A) is much more distinguished than the other; the Liberal candidate, (E), is personally attractive, and on some matters (international relations in particular) leans quite strongly to the Labour side. The Communist vote (for D) consists, as usual, of a fringe of miscellaneous malcontents and a small nucleus of those who follow the party line whatever it is; in this instance, 'the line' demands a close alliance with Labour, even though Labour repudiates it.

The ballot-paper of an average Conservative voter might perhaps be marked as follows:—

A	(Labour)	–
B	(Conservative)	1
C	(Conservative)	2
D	(Communist)	–
E	(Liberal)	4
F	(Labour)	–
G	(Conservative)	3

(He might perhaps, if he greatly preferred the personality of one of the Labour candidates, A, to that of F, go so far as to give his fifth preference to A). This might perhaps prove to be the most usual Conservative pattern, but (as will be seen later) many variations are possible, even among 'good' Conservatives.

Suppose then that for the three seats 8,000 votes are cast: the Droop quota will be $\frac{8,000}{3+1} + 1 = 2,001$. The first count is a count of first preference votes only: as a matter of convenience in later counts the first preference votes are sorted into bundles according to the different patterns of later preferences, so that there is a separate bundle ready counted, for each pattern—B1 C2 G3 E4, or (a possible Labour pattern) A1 F2 D3 E4, or (an alternative Labour pattern), A1 F2 E4 D3, and so on. This saves time and trouble in the later stages.

The count of first preferences might be:—

First Count

A	(Labour)	1,900
*B	(Conservative)	2,500
C	(Conservative)	800
D	(Communist)	500
E	(Liberal)	1,000
F	(Labour)	600
G	(Conservative)	700
		8,000

On this count, only B has secured the quota of 2,001: B is declared elected, and the next problem is what to do with the 499 votes which he does not 'need'. These are available for casting in favour of some other candidate: but which of his 2,500 votes are the ones that he does not 'need'? In our first 'model' it was the latecomers who voted again in the 'second round'; but it has never seemed right in a preference system simply to transfer the votes counted last, and there are two alternative methods. One is to take a random sample of 499 out of the 2,500 papers, and to look at the second preferences in these; another, which is simpler in practice and is just as fair, is to look at the second preferences of *all* the 2,500 papers, count the total for each candidate, and give each candidate $\frac{499}{2,500}$ of the votes he thus receives. The second preferences of the Conservative B might divide into:—

A	(Labour)	100
C	(Conservative)	1,500
D	(Communist)	Nil
E	(Liberal)	250
F	(Labour)	50
G	(Conservative)	600
		2,500

There are then available for redistribution (taking $\dfrac{499}{2,500}$ as $= \dfrac{1}{5}$, which is exact enough for our present purpose: greater precision is quite easy for a clerk with a slide rule):

A	20
C	300
D	Nil
E	50
F	10
G	120
	———
	500
	———

and the result on this round will be:—

Second Count	A	(Labour)	1,900 + 20 = 1,920
	C	(Conservative)	800 + 300 = 1,100
	D	(Communist)	500 + 0 = 500
	E	(Liberal)	1,000 + 50 = 1,050
	F	(Labour)	600 + 10 = 610
	G	(Conservative)	700 + 120 = 820
			5,500 + 500 = 6,000

No one has attained the quota and therefore no one but B is yet elected: the next step is to reject the candidate with the smallest number of votes at this stage, who is D, the Communist. Let us assume (what would not always be the case in practice[1]) that all his voters have used their second preference, and have done so as follows (the party-liners give second preference to Labour, and there is a small 'scatter' of votes by the 'lunatic fringe'):—

A	(Labour)	300
C	(Conservative)	20
E	(Liberal)	20
F	(Labour)	140
G	(Conservative)	20
		———
		500
		———

[1] If all preferences are not used, there are fewer votes in the count, and therefore the quota has to be recalculated for the remaining seats: this presents no difficulty. There are, however, systems which declare a ballot-paper invalid unless it puts all the candidates, or a specified number of candidates (say three), in order of preference.

There then follows:—

Third Count	*A	(Labour)	1,920 + 300	=	2,220
	C	(Conservative)	1,100 + 20	=	1,120
	E	(Liberal)	1,050 + 20	=	1,070
	F	(Labour)	610 + 140	=	750
	G	(Conservative)	820 + 20	=	840

$$5,500 + 500 = 6,000$$

A is elected, but the other four candidates are still fairly close together and it may need several more counts to decide who gets the third seat. There is some choice here in making rules about procedure; for instance, whether to distribute next A's surplus votes, or to eliminate the second Labour candidate F, who is now running last, or to do both at once on the same count. For the sake of fullness in illustration, let us take the first method.

A has 219 votes more than he needs. We now look at the *second* preferences of the original 1,900 who voted for him; the *third* preferences of those who voted for B first placing A second, since A inherited 20 votes from B on the second count; the *third* preferences of D, since A inherited over 300 votes from D on the third count. Let us then make the following assumptions, to some extent simplified.

A's second preferences are as follows:—

C	(Conservative)	nil			
D	(Communist)	250:	since D has been eliminated we allow these voters their *third* preference: and this is included in the figures for:—		
E	(Liberal)	550 +	50 from D	=	600
F	(Labour)	1,100 +	200 from D	=	1,300
G	(Conservative)	nil +	nil	=	nil

$$1,900$$

It follows that of the 219 (let us call it 220) votes to be redistributed a proportion of $\frac{1,900}{2,220}$ falls to be redistributed in this ratio of 600/1,300. There are thus 188 votes available. These votes then go in the proportions indicated, $\frac{6}{19}$ to the Liberal, $\frac{13}{19}$ to the second Labour candidate, 59 and 129.

The number of Communist third preferences to be redistributed is

$\dfrac{300}{2,220}$ of 220—let us say 30: the number of Conservative third prefer-

ences (from B) is $\dfrac{20}{2,220}$ of 220—let us say 2. To avoid too much com-

plication let us assume that all the third preferences of the Communists went to the second Labour candidate, and so did those of the few eccentrics who placed B (Conservative) first and A (Labour) second, perhaps because of B's great national reputation.

The result of these proceedings is therefore

Fourth	C	(Conservative)	1,120 + nil + nil	= 1,120
Count	E	(Liberal)	1,070 + 59 + nil	= 1,129
	F	(Labour)	750 + 129 + 30 + 2	= 911
	G	(Conservative)	840 + nil + nil	= 840
			3,780 + 220	= 4,000

No one is yet elected, and the next step is therefore to eliminate the weaker of the two remaining Conservatives and redistribute his 840 votes by looking at the *second* preferences for C, E and F, *third* (or later) preferences if second (or later) preferences had been for the candidates successful or eliminated, A, B and D. Let us suppose that the result is to give 600 votes to C, 200 to E, 40 to F. Deadlock still continues:—

Fifth Count	C	(Conservative)	1,120 + 600 = 1,720
	E	(Liberal)	1,129 + 200 = 1,329
	F	(Labour)	911 + 40 = 951
			3,160 + 840 = 4,000

But it is certain that the matter will be settled by one further count.

F, the weakest candidate is now eliminated, the second or later preferences set free are redistributed, and either C or E must reach the quota. The procedure is complicated because F's 951 votes consist of 600 first preferences, 10 preferences allocated after the success of B, 140 after the withdrawal of D, 161 after the success of A, and 40 'new' votes; but the arithmetic is not difficult. The effect, as will be seen, is in the last resort to give the seat which is in doubt between Conservative and Liberal to the candidate favoured by those who voted for the second Labour man but could not get him in. Probably most of them prefer Liberal to Conservative, and the result will therefore be the election of 1 Conservative, 1 Labour, and 1 Liberal member in a constituency where there were 4,000 Conservative first preferences, 2,500 Labour, and 1,000 Liberal first preferences.

This may seem a paradoxical result of what we are looking for in proportionality in terms of *parties*[1]: but this is not the aim of the system, which seeks to give preference to *candidates* who have more support, whether as party members or as individuals, over candidates who have less support. Our example pictured a situation in which party allegiance was important, but not absolute, and in this situation the personal preferences of individuals carried a Liberal home. The system is designed to reflect accurately the attitudes of the voters: it is 'proportional' in this sense, not in the allocation of seats to parties in accordance with first preference votes: that sort of proportionality is aimed at (and can be secured) only by list systems of voting.

The example given here required six counts to decide the issue in a three-member constituency: this is a fairly long but not unusually long contest. In the Oxford University contest in the general election of 1935 it took three counts to elect two members, one of them an orthodox Conservative, the other an unorthodox one, Sir Alan Herbert, who defeated a Labour Party candidate and a second orthodox Conservative, by gaining second preferences from both the Conservative and the Labour sides. Another well-known example is that of the constituency of Cork City in the Irish General Election of 1948, in which fifteen counts were required to elect five members.[2]

3. *Criteria of Voting Systems*

As we have seen in §1 of Chapter VII, the first problem in assessing the advantages and disadvantages of a particular form of voting is to decide what are our criteria of success and failure: different criteria give different verdicts. In a practical situation decisions of this kind are argued, and in the end taken, on the basis of multiple criteria: no one in practice thinks that electoral systems serve one purpose only, and political debate about them is by nature extremely confused. There is good sense in this, but for theoretical discussion it is desirable to set out criteria separately, and to balance one against another. This is a convenient point in our argument at which to do this, because these criteria were first worked out in a sophisticated way in the middle of the nineteenth century, about the time when the S.T.V. system was invented.

There are eight main criteria:—

(a) *Quality of members.* Does the system secure the election of members of good quality? The idea of 'good quality' is of course not unambiguous, as we saw when discussing 'quality franchises' in Chapter III, but it is in a general way clear what it means.

[1] Even in terms of parties there would probably be greater proportionality if there were more seats to fill.
[2] The first example is given in detail in *The Ayes Have It* by A. P. Herbert: the second in Ch. III of *Voting in Democracies* by Enid Lakeman and J. D. Lambert. Both books are recommended to readers interested in the S.T.V. system.

(b) *The member and his constituency.* Does the system secure the election of members qualified to speak for those who supported them, and in close touch with the electorate? In other words, are the members good 'constituency men'?

(c) *A collectively effective assembly.* Does the system make it possible for the assembly elected to do the business required of it? This business is different in different political systems; different things are required from the American Senate and House of Representatives, which do not choose the executive, from the Swiss Federal Assembly which chooses an executive to act independently of the two Houses, and from the directly elected Houses in Britain and France, from which emerge cabinets continuously dependent on them for support. In this last case, the assembly must be capable of maintaining a stable majority or it will produce unstable cabinets. Whether there is a stable majority depends on the working of the party system: and this criterion may resolve itself into another. Does the voting system tend to strengthen or weaken the party system? Does it promote party discipline among the electorate and in the assembly? How does it affect the number of parties and the possibility of lasting coalitions between them?

(d) *Reflection of opinion.* Does the system fairly reflect opinion? How we construe this depends partly on our attitude to (c) and (d). Is the opinion to be reflected the organised opinion of disciplined parties? Or the opinion of the individual voter on complicated issues presented to him without prior simplification by a control between parties?

(e) *Attitude of electors in voting.* Does the system encourage voters to take the right attitude to their own choice? Does it 'educate' them in the practice of democracy? We have seen (p. 53) that there is some ambiguity here too: is it right that the voter should be given a chance to express all the ramifications of his attitude to a complex situation? Or should he be forced to take a narrow but effective decision by limiting his freedom of choice to a small number of pre-determined options?

(f) *Public confidence.* Does the system inspire public confidence in its fairness and effectiveness? This involves public belief in the competence and impartiality of electoral administration, and some public understanding of the relation between votes and results.

(g) *By-elections.* Vacancies are bound to occur during the tenure of office of a large assembly, and they cannot be left unfilled without effects on the balance of power in the assembly. How are they to be filled? In some systems (in many list systems of P.R. for instance) the general election produces lists of 'reserves', placed in order, who can step into the assembly without a further election if a member of their party falls out. In other systems it is necessary to have by-elections, and a series of individual elections therefore takes place at unpredictable intervals between general elections. This has the advantage of giving some indication of the current state of opinion: but to secure this the system must be such that it admits by-elections without great administrative inconvenience and without distorting the process of choice.

(h) *Political possibility*. Finally, there is a criterion of a rather different kind. Methods of voting nowadays are rarely imposed from outside upon a political system: this has happened in the development of elections in colonies and of plebiscites in occupied territories, but these occasions grow rarer and must be treated as exceptions. A voting system is usually created by an act within the political system to which it belongs. An existing ruler must be convinced, a majority must be found within an existing assembly: it is useless to propose a voting system for the defence of interests which are not powerful enough to secure the introduction of the system, unless of course they can find allies of greater strength. We shall return at the end of Chapter X to this question of voting systems in relation to the defence of a regime.

Some of the ambiguities of these criteria have been indicated, and much more could be written about them. But it will be best to illustrate them in the course of discussion of the effects of particular systems.

4. *Assessment of S.T.V.*

It should be said at the outset that evidence about the use of the S.T.V. system in large political units is still very limited. It has been used for elections to the main popular assembly only in the Republic of Ireland, which has a population of about 3 million, and in Tasmania, which has a population of 300,000. It is used for elections to second chambers in the Commonwealth of Australia and in New South Wales, and on a limited scale in some parliamentary and local elections elsewhere. Discussion therefore proceeds on the basis of general probabilities, and of experience of the system in smaller units, which is considerable.

It is agreed on all hands that the system is much the most elegant device available for enabling individuals to express themselves through the electoral process in such a way that the outcome of voting bears a logical relationship to the votes cast. At some points, however, the logic is drawn rather fine. When it comes to second and third preferences, it may often happen that what is reckoned is not the individual vote of any specific elector, but a vote derived by sums in proportion from the votes of a large number of electors. There is no exact answer (in our example) to the question exactly which individuals it was whose votes put in the candidates A and F, Labour and Liberal, who were ultimately chosen. The votes of practically all electors played some part, including those of electors whose ballot papers suggested that their opinion of A and F was not very high. But if the problem is set, this is perhaps the least illogical way to solve it. The dispute is not over the logic but over the practical effects of this form of expression.

(a) *Quality of members.* The tendency of the system (like that of primary elections—p. 41) is to give more opportunity to the voter to express an opinion about the merits of individual candidates. In a constituency such as that in our example it can be made plain whom the voters think to be best of the the Conservative candidates, and an independent Conservative rejected by the party machine might have stood as a candidate without splitting the party vote. The electorate gains freedom in the choice of members, at the expense of the parties: whether this means better members depends on the quality of the electorate and on their sources of information about the candidates.

(b) *The member and his constituency.* It is agreed that multi-member constituencies are necessary; the three-member constituency used in our example was too small to be altogether satisfactory. In consequence, a member is not closely attached to a fairly small locality, as he is under a single-member constituency system: it may be that instead of having a strong local attachment he builds up a personal and political following, with which he is associated just as closely, but in rather a different way. J. S. Mill thought that Thomas Hare's system would create a House of Commons elected by the electorate as a whole in which each member would have his own 'constituency' consisting of those whose votes sent him to Parliament, his personal supporters perhaps scattered over the whole country. Mill's system of voting without territorial sub-divisions is clearly impracticable except in a very small country: but perhaps the same sort of thing might happen within (say) a five-member constituency. One solution proposed is that the five-member constituency should be divided into five 'wards', and a member assigned to each of them, by choice or by lot: but this is perhaps too artificial a device to produce the desired effect.

(c) *A collectively effective assembly.* The S.T.V. system is often criticised on the ground that it may wreck the stability of the executive in countries where the executive depends for its existence on continuous support in the elected assembly. There is no doubt that the theoretical tendency (indeed part of the purpose) of S.T.V. is to weaken the grip of parties on the mechanism of elections. It should do so for two reasons: because it makes it relatively easy for small parties to establish and maintain themselves, and because it enables the elector to express his choice between the candidates offered to him by his own party. S.T.V. therefore tends to break up a system of two parties, and to weaken discipline within each party in the Assembly and in the country.

It may thus make responsible cabinet government more difficult: but this is no more than a tendency, which may be counter-balanced in various ways. The system of voting is not the only reason for the emergence of two great parties in some countries but not in others, and the tendency to party domination may prove stronger than the effects of S.T.V. The climate of opinion in the country may be strongly opposed to Cabinet instability, and it may therefore be possible for an assembly with several parties and much freedom of speech to produce a majority coherent enough to support a Cabinet for long periods.

The evidence is limited. In Ireland, de Valera reduced the size of constituencies under S.T.V. and thus increased the bias against small parties. Out of this and out of Irish traditions and personalities has arisen for the present a curious balance between de Valera's party on one side, a coalition of small parties on the other. Cabinets in Ireland have not been conspicuously unstable: and there are countries (the Scandinavian countries in particular) which have stable Cabinets in spite of the existence of several equally balanced parties whose position is protected by some form of P.R. under the list system.

(d) *Reflection of opinion.* The system undoubtedly reflects individual opinions as well as any system can, within the administrative limits set by the huge size of modern electorates. A counter-argument can only be constructed on this point by insisting that in politics what counts is organised opinion: not the sort of opinion which expresses itself in answer to the questionnaires of the 'Gallup poll', but opinion shaped by party organisation into an effective political instrument, associating known leaders, an alert body of henchmen, coherent principles and an agreed programme of action. This is a crucial point in debate about mass democracy: the case for political parties is strong, but it is also possible to reverse the argument and to suggest that since party organisation is hostile to free speech within the party, it is as likely to block public opinion as to canalise it.

(e) *The attitude of electors.* J. S. Mill, the greatest of all advocates of S.T.V., laid most stress on the educational function of democracy. For him the main merit of representative government was that it produced an 'active self-helping type'[1] of man (and woman) more effectively than any other sort of government. Most people would agree about this: but unfortunately the 'educational' effect may be secured in two different ways, not always completely compatible. First, men and women become better politically by practice in exercising their wits in the subtleties of politics, by adjusting their judgments to the facts as they know them. Secondly, men and women become better in rather a different sense if they are made to share in responsibility: to take decisions which are effective in the sense that the decider must suffer in his own person if he has chosen wrong. It is scarcely in dispute that S.T.V. is more 'educational' than 'first past the post' voting in the first of these senses: it sets the elector a more interesting and varied problem. But the single member constituency system probably has the advantage

[1] *Representative Government* (World's Classics ed.) at p. 195.

in the second sense: experience is lacking, but it is less likely that under S.T.V. an election can become in effect the direct choice of a government to which the chooser must submit for the next few years.

(f) *Public confidence*. The weakness of the S.T.V. system in this respect is secondary rather than direct. It is not hard for experienced people to administer, and the logic of the arithmetical processes involved can be explained in fairly simple terms, at least to people who are interested in that sort of logic and take pleasure in the construction of an argument. But such people are relatively few in number, and the average voter under S.T.V. is not likely to understand the system fully. It is impossible to judge without experience how important this difficulty would be in practice. Many would be prepared to put down an order of preference on the ballot paper and to take it on trust from those who know better that their vote in some way finally becomes effective: but the relative complexity of the system means that it is vulnerable to attack by unfriendly persons who wish to make fun of it. In this as in so many things, the decisive factor is the growth of habit and tradition.

(g) *By-elections* are essential, as the system (unlike list systems of P.R.) cannot fairly be used to designate 'reserve' members to fill casual vacancies. This means in practice that a large constituency normally electing perhaps five members by S.T.V. must vote in a by-election to choose one member, either by the simple plurality system, or by a second ballot, or by the alternative vote. There is some minor inconvenience in this, but no real difficulty.

(h) *Political Possibility*. Judged by these arguments alone S.T.V. is certainly a valuable 'tool in the bag', more suitable in some circumstances than in others, but not to be rejected out of hand. Its weakness in terms of practical politics is that it is difficult to induce established political parties to support it, because there is good reason to believe that it will be hostile to their interests. A strong two-party system is most easily maintained under single-member plurality voting, and where that system exists the two largest parties (even though otherwise irreconcilable) generally unite to support it. In a multi-party system parties find it easier to preserve internal discipline under some variant of the list system than under S.T.V.: the best disciplined parties therefore defend list systems, and the odds are on their success. It is more likely that the two strongest of them will combine to introduce some form of plurality voting than that there will be a combination of parties to go over from the list system to S.T.V. S.T.V. where it exists gains most of its support from the smaller parties and from the sentiment of individual voters. Its existence in Ireland is for this reason a little precarious: its introduction elsewhere is unlikely, except in elections not deemed important by organised political parties.

CHAPTER IX

List Systems of Proportional Representation

1. *Introductory*

A 'list' system is one in which the voter is invited to choose not between individuals but between lists of candidates, each of which is sponsored by a party or by some other organisation. It is in practice a system of 'voting the party ticket', but that phrase may be misleading in this context because it originated in rather different circumstances. 'To vote the ticket' means in the U.S.A. to vote for the candidates sponsored by the party in a series of separate single-member elections held simultaneously: under the old 'long ballot' system an American voter might be called upon to enter the polling-station and cast separate votes in elections for perhaps thirty different offices, ranging from President and Vice-President of the U.S.A., Senator, and Congressman, through a series of State officials down to the level of the (imaginary) local 'dog-catcher'. In such circumstances most voters take their line from the party and vote as directed by it: but occasionally a strong candidate attracts votes of his own and 'runs ahead of the ticket'. Some similar phenomena may be observed in the operation of the list system; but the latter differs in principle because it is one of voting in multi-member constituencies in which each party submits on its list as many candidates as there are seats, and the voter casts only one vote, a vote for the list which he prefers.

List systems may be associated with 'first past the post' voting or with some form of majority voting, and more will be said of this in the next chapter. But, in general, opinion recoils from a system which enables one party to 'scoop the pool' in a multi-member constituency by a bare majority, or even by a simple plurality of votes: and list voting is almost always associated with formulae for distributing seats among parties in proportion to the votes cast for each list.

This is a type of proportional representation which became important a generation after the invention of S.T.V. Perhaps the critical event in its development was the decision to adopt it in Belgium in 1899, because it appeared there to have real political success. In the last quarter of the nineteenth century, under a system of majority voting with a second ballot, there had been violent and dangerous oscillations between Liberal and Catholic parties, which also represented the linguistic division between Walloon and Fleming. After the adoption of the list system these oscillations were reduced; Cabinets had weaker majorities and shorter lives, but there was much less danger of permanent and irreconcilable division within the country.

There were perhaps two reasons why during this period the system suited political developments in Western and Central Europe: it was proportional, and therefore did not stress latent tendencies to sharp divisions between Right and Left, Catholic and Marxist; it gave the party managers much influence on the choice of individual members to be returned by the votes cast for the party, and thus strengthened party discipline.

The list system therefore became the natural and inevitable system of voting in two rather different political environments, Austria-Hungary and its successor states—and Switzerland in some ways belongs to this group—were internally split by a series of deep divisions between their citizens, divisions of language, religion, and economic status, and in them there evolved party systems in which each party acted for a particular clientele, often closely associated in other kinds of organisation as well. One can imagine a state in which there would be a Slovak Catholic Peasant Party, a Slovak Catholic Workers Party, a Slovak Catholic Business Man's Party, a Hungarian Catholic Peasant Party and so on; and each of these political organisations would have associated with it a group of Trade Unions and Trade Associations, a group of Cooperatives, an organisation of schools and teachers, and (in some form) a sectarian religious organisation, providing for its members certain social services of a simple kind. Such states were in effect plural societies, held together partly by the bureaucratic regime, partly by complex economic ties; the list system worked well so long as its function was to provide a Parliament which represented but did not govern, standing over against the central bureaucracy and taking no responsibility for it. When the Habsburg hand was withdrawn, it was impossible to find a new regime for the whole area, and it was not easy to do so even within each of the new national states, which were themselves deeply divided. Czechoslovakia, Austria, and Hungary might, but for violent external pressure, have succeeded in evolving stable forms of democracy within the framework of the list system and of the old system of parties, somewhat simplified. Switzerland has done so, but through a long course of political development which is peculiarly its own.

The list system has also become the usual form of voting in the stable democracies of Northern Europe, Belgium, Holland, Denmark, Norway, Sweden, Finland. There are substantial differences between them; Belgium and Holland are troubled by confessional differences, Belgium and to a slight extent Finland have problems of language. But in each country there have evolved a relatively small number of stable parties—the Scandinavian pattern (where almost all are Lutherans of the State Church) is that of Conservative, Liberal, Labour, Peasant; these parties maintain their own position through the list system, are in some respects irreconcilable, but are in the habit of working together, so that coalition or minority cabinets hold office for long periods, often undisturbed by the very slight changes in representation which take place at elections.

In this sort of situation proportional representation is compatible with stability, and its abolition is in these countries unthinkable. The position is not so happy in France, Western Germany and Italy, where controversy about systems of voting has become an integral part of the political struggle, and problems have arisen to which we recur in the next chapter. It is enough to say here that list systems of P.R. though used in these three great countries cannot be regarded (at least as yet) as an integral part of their political life.

2. *Methods of Calculation*

Nothing could be simpler than the first principle of the system. Suppose a constituency in which 24,000 votes are cast for four party lists contesting five seats, and suppose a very simple distribution of votes:—

List A	13,500
List B	4,500
List C	4,500
List D	1,500
	24,000

It seems easy to say that Party D get no seats, and that the other parties divide the seats in proportion to their votes, 3 : 1 : 1. The seats given to each party are then filled by taking names from each list in the order in which they have been placed on it by the party.

The trouble is that things never in practice work out with such simplicity. One is almost certain to get a less tidy distribution: for instance:—

List A	8,700
List B	6,800
List C	5,200
List D	3,300
	24,000

One must then attempt to distribute five seats in rather ugly proportions:—

$$\text{List A gets } \frac{5 \times 87}{240} = \text{(to 3 places only) } 1\cdot813$$

$$\text{List B } \text{,, } \frac{5 \times 68}{240} = \text{,, \quad ,, \quad ,, } 1\cdot416$$

$$\text{List C } \text{,, } \frac{5 \times 52}{240} = \text{,, \quad ,, \quad ,, } 1\cdot008$$

$$\text{List D } \text{,, } \frac{5 \times 33}{240} = \text{,, \quad ,, \quad ,, } \cdot687$$

What next? This looks like a proportion of 2: 1: 1: 0; but who is to get the fifth seat? The result will look queer, whether we give it to A, to B, to C or to D.

Two alternative methods have been evolved for giving unreal precision to the arithmetic involved. These are as follows:—

(a) *Highest average.* The first method is that known as 'P.R. by the highest average'; and also as the d'Hondt rule, after its Belgian inventor. The principle of it is that the seats are allocated one by one, and each goes to the list which would have the highest average number of votes per seat if it received the seat in question. The formula for getting this result is that at each allocation each list's original total of votes is divided by one more than the number of seats that list has already won, in order to discover what its average would be if it won the seat in question.

At the first allocation no list has yet won a seat, so the divisor for each list is 1, and the 'averages' are therefore the lists' original totals.

List A	8,700★
List B	6,800
List C	5,200
List D	3,300

List A has the highest average and therefore wins the seat.

For the allocation of the second seat the divisor for List A is 2 (i.e. one seat already gained plus 1), the divisor for each of the other lists remains 1, and List B gets the seat; as follows:—

List	Total Votes	Divisor	Average
A	8,700	2	4,350
B	6,800	1	6,800★
C	5,200	1	5,200
D	3,300	1	3,300

For the allocation of the third seat the divisor for list A remains 2, that for list B becomes 2, and that for the other lists remains 1. List C therefore gets this third seat; as follows:—

List	Total Votes	Divisor	Average
A	8,700	2	4,350
B	6,800	2	3,400
C	5,200	1	5,200★
D	3,300	1	3,300

For the allocation of the fourth seat the divisors for lists A and B remain 2, that for list C becomes 2, and that for list D remains 1. List A therefore gets the fourth seat; as follows:—

List	Total Votes	Divisor	Average
A	8,700	2	4,350★
B	6,800	2	3,400
C	5,200	2	2,600
D	3,300	1	3,300

For the allocation of the fifth seat the divisor for list A becomes 3, but the other divisors are unchanged, and List B gets the seat; as follows:—

List	Total Votes	Divisor	Average
A	8,700	3	2,900
B	6,800	2	3,400★
C	5,200	2	2,600
D	3,300	1	3,300

Thus, in the end, lists A and B have 2 seats each, list C has 1 seat, and list D has none.

Such a result may appear unfair. Why should list B have two seats although it has only three-quarters as many votes as List A, which also has two seats? And why should list D have no seats, although it has almost half as many voters as list B, which has two seats? In the allocation of seats the system has favoured the larger lists at the expense of the smaller.

(b) *Greatest Remainder*. To deal with criticisms of this kind an alternative method has been devised: P.R. by the greatest remainder. The principles of this method is to calculate an electoral quotient (not the same as the Droop quota) by dividing total votes cast by seats to be awarded: then to give each list as many seats as its poll contains the quotient; finally, if any seats remain, to allocate them successively between the competing lists according to the sizes of the remainder obtained by deducting from the original vote of each list the votes it has already 'used' to gain a seat or seats by means of the quotient.

The quotient is obtained by dividing the grand total of votes by the number of seats, and therefore in our example it is $\frac{24,000}{5} = 4,800$ (the Droop quota would be $\frac{24,000}{5 + 1} + 1 = 4,001$). The rest of the calculation can be presented as follows:—

List	Votes (V)	Seats (S) won by quotient (Q)	$(S \times Q)$	Remainder $(V) - (S \times Q)$
A	8,700	1	4,800	3,900
B	6,800	1	4,800	2,000
C	5,200	1	4,800	400
D	3,300	0	—	3,300

The list with the largest remainder is A, which therefore wins a second seat (the fourth of the 5 to be allocated). The list with the next largest remainder is D, which therefore wins its first seat, the last to be allocated. Thus in the end List A has 2 seats, and each of the other lists has 1 each. Therefore by using the greatest remainder instead of the highest average we have given list D a seat at the expense of list B. The system has favoured a smaller party at the expense of a larger one.

But if the party sponsoring list B were composed of two fairly equal factions, or if it could rely absolutely on the readiness of its supporters to do as they were told, it could profit from this to defeat the object of the system. Let us assume that it managed to divide its votes almost equally between two lists, (B1 and B2). Then the results would be as follows:—

List	Votes (V)	Seats (S) won by Quotient (Q)	$(S \times Q)$	Remainder $(V) - (S \times Q)$
A	8,700	1	4,800	3,900
B1	3,450	0	—	3,450
B2	3,350	0	—	3,350
C	5,200	1	4,800	400
D	3,300	0	—	3,300

The third seat to be allocated would go to List A, which has the largest remainder, the fourth seat would go to list B1 and the fifth seat would go to list B2. Thus the party sponsoring the two B lists would gain two seats and the party sponsoring list D would gain none.

3. *Variations of the system*

There are two other vulnerable points at which changes can be made in the system to meet criticism, without sacrifice of principle.

(a) *Preferential voting and* panachage. It is a standing reproach that list systems give great power to party machines because the voters are given no voice in the choice of individual members: the parties of course pay some attention to popular appeal in putting forward candidates, but in effect the voters choose between parties, the parties choose the members.

There is no technical difficulty in permitting the voter to choose on the same ballot paper between individuals as well as between parties, though the calculations which follow may be complicated:—

(i) *Preferential voting within one list.* One alternative is to maintain the rule that the allocation of seats between parties is determined solely by votes cast for lists, but to allow the voter to choose the order of names within the list which he favours. There are then in a sense two separate elections on the same piece of paper: the first to allocate seats to parties, the second (limited to the voters of each successful party) to determine which of the party candidates are to get the seats allocated to the party. This second selection can be conducted on any of the individual systems of voting described in Chapters VII and VIII, but probably S.T.V. is the best and the usual system for the purpose. The freedom of choice thus given to the voters may be ineffective in practice, because preferential voting cannot very well be made compulsory, and those who put no marks of preference opposite the names of individual candidates must be assumed to accept the order given by the party; this is much the simplest thing for the average elector to do.[1]

(ii) Panachage *between lists.* This variation can be taken further, so that in theory it changes the character of the system, by allowing the voter to mix party lists together; in a seven-member constituency (for example) an elector would have seven votes (or one vote divisible into sevenths), and could divide his vote between parties in any ratio he pleased, such as 5 : 1 : 1. Voters are not likely to do this except to support an individual on some list other than that of their own party: and *panachage* is not of any value unless combined with preferential voting, the right to favour an individual. But even so the first stage in voting is still the allocation of votes between lists: in the example above, the imaginary voter has given five votes to List A, one each to List B and List C, and it is the sum of the votes for each list which determines the number of seats to be shared among its candidates. It is in the second stage that the voter's choice may help the individual candidate whom he favours. In theory, by devices of this kind a list system can be given some of the flexibility of the S.T.V. system: but practice lags

[1] The French electoral laws of 1946 and 1951 provided for preferential voting but in practice negatived it by stipulating that it should operate only if half a list's ballot papers were changed.

behind theory, because the vote for the party comes first, and there are relatively few voters[1] who wish to break away from it, especially if the effect may be to benefit not the man of their choice, but another party. For instance, under the French electoral law of 1951 in the constituency of Herault, 7,000 voters of other parties signified their support for one of the Socialist candidates, M. Jules Moch, a national figure who had as Minister of the Interior played a great part in resisting Communism. But M. Moch would have been returned in any case, and the result of his popularity was to give an additional seat to the Socialist party, which went to the third man on their list.

(b) *Regional and national pools of votes.* Both the systems described in the last section (highest average and greatest remainder) have the weakness in proportional theory that there is always an 'unrepresented' remainder of votes in each constituency which may be as high as $\left(\dfrac{\text{Votes cast}}{\text{Seats to be filled} + 1} \right)$—one less than the Droop quota. This remainder could be proportionately reduced by increasing the size of the constituency; but there is a limit to what is thought tolerable in this respect, even under list systems, and constituencies usually have not more than 8-10 seats (the largest known to the author had 38). The unrepresented remainder may therefore be substantial, if added together for the country as a whole—perhaps 10% of the electorate; minorities below this size may go without spokesmen and without votes with which to bargain, a matter which may be quite serious where each party is organised specifically to cater for its own clientele, and does not (as do the major British parties) cast its net wide to catch the 'floating voter' and 'marginal' interest.

There is no technical difficulty in dealing with the problem by arranging that all parties, large and small (but generally there is some provision for a minimum, for instance that a party is not further considered unless it gains at least x% of the votes cast in constituencies for which it has entered lists) may carry forward unused remainders to a number of regional pools, to each of which seats are allocated in proportion to the votes entering it: and from the regional pools remainders can be carried forward to a national pool. This sort of system was used for the 'surplus' votes of all parties, large as well as small, under the Weimar Republic in Germany. It certainly helped to strengthen party bureaucracy and to increase the number of very small parties represented in the Reichstag, but it has attracted more blame than it deserves. Its form suggests an obsession with impractical subtleties, and perhaps this spirit was characteristic of the constitution-makers of 1919: but if harm was done it was by the spirit, not by the form, which

---

[1] About 7% in the French general election of 1951.

had little effect one way or the other on the underlying problems of German politics.

4. *Assessment of the list systems.*

Much has been said in passing about the effects of these systems, and it is only necessary to summarise this now, in relation to the points listed in Chapter VIII.

(a) *Quality of members.* The choice of members, even where preferential voting is allowed, depends largely on the parties. These are not wholly unresponsive to public opinion, but it is primarily their character which determines the character of members.

(b) *The member and his constituency.* The effects are like those of any multi-member constituency system: the member represents primarily not a locality as a whole, but a group of like-minded people. This can be modified slightly by allocating individual members to single-member districts: it is intensified if the system is run on the basis that there shall (for instance) be one member for every 50,000 voters, regardless of locality, so that regional and national pools play a relatively important part.

(c) *A collectively effective assembly.* These systems tend to strengthen discipline within parties, and also to fix the number of parties at more than two. They do not in general appear to increase the number of parties indefinitely: one could devise a system likely to encourage this, but most systems represent a compromise which gives existing parties some power to resist splits and the creation of new parties. This situation makes for stable coalition or minority cabinets if the parties are capable of working together, for chaos if they are not; the roots of such attitudes lie much deeper in the structure of the political community.

(d) *Reflection of opinion.* List systems in their most elaborate forms are sensitive devices for registering in the composition of the assembly the amount of support given to each party by the voters. They do not register opinion in any other sense; indeed, they scarcely recognise its political existence. This is part of a consistent view of the place of parties in the state.

(e) *Attitude of electors to voting.* The effects of the system here perhaps lie between those of single-member constituencies and those of S.T.V. The subtleties of expression open to the voter are (usually) more limited than under S.T.V.: his choice is not so directly related to the choice of a government as under the 'first past the post' system, since governments are generally fixed by compromise between parties joining a coalition majority.

(f) *Public confidence.* These systems though rigid are relatively plain, except when attempts are made to give real effect to preferential voting and *panachage*. Probably most electors find them simpler to follow than S.T.V. and the mixed systems described in Chapter X. The most obvious line of attack is based on sarcasms not about complexity but about party bureaucracy and about indecisive coalitions of wire-pullers.

(g) *By-elections*. Under list systems it is possible to dispense with by-elections altogether, by allowing the next candidate on the relevant list to take the place of the member who has dropped out. This is generally done, but if by-elections are wanted it is easy to hold them, subject to the same difficulty as that of by-elections under S.T.V., that there is some inconvenience in electing one member in a large multi-member constituency, and that the result cannot be proportional, like the rest of the system, but must favour the strongest party, even though the seat had been fairly awarded to a weaker party at the general election.

(h) *Political Possibility*. It might be said that list systems are all too possible. Like the 'first past the post' system, they create vested interests which tend to maintain them; their virtues and their defects perpetuate themselves equally, and they are likely to remain the basis of one of the main forms of Western democracy.

CHAPTER X

Electoral Engineering

1. *Introductory*

This chapter deals mainly with the recent history of voting systems in France, Germany and Italy. It is not part of the plan of this book to explain any electoral system fully in its political context: this could only be done by a different kind of study, and the references to these three countries here are necessarily superficial. It is, however, essential to include them, as the future of free elections in Western Europe (and therefore in the world, perhaps) depends largely on the success or failure of these political experiments, and on the world's estimate of their ethical standing. The questions raised are deep and difficult ones.

The common factor in these three countries (which have together a population of 140 million people, two-thirds of the population of continental Europe outside the zone of Marxist influence) is that all have experienced a period of responsible cabinet government under free elections; in all, this period was ended by violent party struggles and a totalitarian regime; and in all, 'free elections' were restored after the defeat of Hitler in 1945. France lived under responsible cabinet government from 1871 to 1940, Italy from 1861 to 1922, Germany from 1918 to 1933; all these regimes were slipshod, unromantic, a little corrupt, but few doubt now that they were immensely superior as ways of life to the Fascist, Nazi and Petainist domination which replaced them. Yet in their revived forms they are perhaps weaker than they were before, since they are threatened on one flank by sentimental memories of the dictatorships, which grow more attractive as they grow more distant, on the other by Communist parties which present themselves as heirs of the great revolutionary tradition in Europe. In this situation certain electoral results may be fatal to the regime. If the extremes together obtain more than half the seats in the Assembly they make democracy impossible; if they obtain even a third of the seats they limit its value, because they force into alliance centre parties which disagree among themselves as much as do the Conservative and Labour parties in Britain, and which ought, if possible, to debate their differences in public and to submit them to decision by the electorate. In this situation, is it ethically right, is it 'democratic', to arrange the system of voting in such a way as to strengthen the 'democratic' parties and to weaken their opponents, in the hope that the forces working against democracy may waste away through under-representation in the Assembly? If it is right, how is it to be done? The technical problem is almost as hard as the ethical one, and we will deal with it first.

An almost infinite number of different 'prescriptions' can be built up out of the elements explained in the preceding chapters, and the systems at present in use are the result of much ingenuity and political bargaining. As a result, none of them is elegant or even consistent; nevertheless, they can be used to illustrate three types of solution, each contrived to meet a particular situation by an adaptation of the list system, the basic electoral system of continental Europe. These solutions can be summarised briefly by saying that there is in France a system of local alliances and a bonus of seats to the list locally successful, as well as a judicious mixture of 'highest average' and 'greatest remainder': in Italy a system of national 'alliances' combined with a bonus of seats to the alliance most successful in the whole election; in Germany, a list system combined with certain features of the single-member constituency system, so as to discourage small parties, increase the solidarity of the majority, and attach at least half the members specifically to a local constituency as well as to a party.

2. France

France emerged from the war with a regime based on uneasy co-operation between Catholic progressives (the M.R.P.), Socialists and Communists, with some support from the remains of the old Radical Party. This coalition was led by General de Gaulle, who can scarcely be called a Conservative, but represented a right wing tradition of energetic government. De Gaulle left the government early in 1946, in disgust with the form of constitution to which the parties were committed: but the rest of the coalition held together long enough to make the compromise constitution finally approved by the French people in October 1946. There was then an election, the first election of the Fourth Republic, under a law which was in essentials the same as the ordinance of 1945 regulating elections to the two constituent assemblies in October 1945 and June 1946. One object of these laws was to strengthen party discipline in general, and in particular to help the governing parties: they provided for a system of proportional representation on the list system with fairly large constituencies and no national or regional pools. In metropolitan France (544 deputies) seats were allocated by the system of highest average, which favours the larger parties; the same system was used in each overseas constituency with at least two seats (a total of 60 seats); for 15 single-member constituencies overseas the 'Anglo-Saxon' system was adopted.

This produced an assembly composed roughly as follows (one must always remember that—except on the Left—party allegiance sits lightly in France, and many members realign themselves during the period of a parliament):

	Seats	Percentage of seats[1]	Percentage of Votes[1]
Communists	166	30·5	28·5
Socialists	90	16·6	17·8
M.R.P.	158	29·0	26·3
Radicals, etc.	60	11·0	14·3
Right wing groups	70	12·9	12·8
Overseas deputies (all shades)	74[2]	—	—
Total	618	—	—

This assembly lived through difficult times: first, 'Tripartisme', the joint government of M.R.P., Socialists and Communists: then (in May 1947) the withdrawal of the Communists, which thrust the point of balance in the Assembly further to the right, and began the effective revival of the centre and right-centre groups: then the wave of emotion in favour of General de Gaulle's *Rassemblement du Peuple Français*, which offered 'strong government' as the answer to Communism. In the late 1940s it seemed clear from the results of local government elections that the next general election (which could not be postponed beyond 1951) would lead to an ungovernable assembly if the old electoral law were still used. The centre parties would lose votes to the extreme right and left, and in addition the rule of the highest average would favour the large parties, the Communists and the R.P.F., against the smaller parties of the centre. There was likely to arise a situation in which no government could be formed without the support either of the Communists or of de Gaulle. Clearly there was a majority in France against both these alternatives: to make a choice between them would mean destruction of the moderate centre, perhaps also civil war and foreign intervention. Hence the parties in control of the government had both selfish and patriotic grounds for seeking a way out. But each party had also its own interest to defend, and the year 1950 was one of extremely intricate, tedious and ill-tempered bargaining over the law to be used for the elections of 1951.

The law adopted had two features important to us here:—

(a) In the Paris area, eight constituencies in the Departments of Seine and Seine-et-Oise, the centre parties felt themselves to be particularly

[1] These figures are for France only.
[2] A further seat for Cochin-China was never filled.

weak: the Communists are strong in the working-class districts of Paris and its industrial suburbs, the middle-class was likely to swing towards de Gaulle. For these seats (75 out of 544 seats in France itself), therefore, the law substituted for the system of highest average the system of the greatest remainder, which favours the smaller parties. Even so, the Communist party and its allies and the R.P.F. secured between them 47 out of the 75 seats.

The same system was adopted in three overseas territories (9 seats) for the same reasons. Here the Communists and R.P.F. secured 6 seats. The other overseas seats (74 altogether) included 23 single-member constituencies contested on the single ballot system; this left 51 seats, and for 30 of these (the Algerian seats) the system was the same as that in provincial France (explained below).[1] For the other 21 colonial seats (8 constituencies) the system used was that of P.R. by the highest average (as in provincial France) but without preferential voting, *panachage*, or *apparentement*. Of these 74 seats 17 went to the R.P.F., the Communists and their allies, 56 to the centre parties.

(b) In the rest of France (95 constituencies, 469 seats out of 544) the centre parties were individually weak but collectively strong. The divisions between these parties assume different patterns in different parts of France: their local rivalries are often intense: but they form together a bulwark of resistance to violent change coming from any quarter. To meet this situation the system of *apparentements* or alliances was adopted. The voter was still to vote for the party of his choice, but alliances could be formed in any constituency between 'national' parties, which were defined as parties presenting lists in at least thirty *départements* (out of a total of 90). This meant in practice the traditional centre parties: it was very unlikely that any new party could fight seriously on so wide a front, the Communists were unacceptable to all as allies, the R.P.F. was less isolated than the Communists but not as capable of alliances as the centre parties. Alliances were made locally, and not by agreement between the national headquarters of the parties, and the pattern varied according to the tactical situation in each constituency. If an alliance (or a single list not belonging to an alliance) secured an absolute majority of the votes in any constituency, it secured all the seats for that constituency, regardless of proportionality. If there was no absolute majority, the seats for the constituency were divided between alliances and isolated lists on the system of highest average—which favours the larger groups, in this instance (it was hoped) the alliances of centre parties. Thereafter the members of an alliance divided between themselves the seats gained in each constituency, by the rule of highest average.

[1] Except that in 21 of them there was no *panachage* or preferential voting.

This system applied to the 95 metropolitan constituencies outside the Paris area; there were alliances in 83 of them (none including the Communists, only 12 including the R.P.F.): and alliances swept the board in 40 constituencies. The result for this part of the election was (in effect):—

	Seats	Percent Seats	Percent Votes
Communists and their allies	72	16·0	24·8
Centre parties	312	66·5	54·5
R.P.F.	85	17·5	20·7

For the whole National Assembly, including the Paris area and the overseas seats, the position was as follows:—

	Seats	Percentage of Seats	Percentage of Votes
Communists	97	17·8	25·9
Socialists	94	17·3	14·5
M.R.P.	82	15·1	12·5
Radicals, etc.	77	14·1	10·0
R.P.F.	107	19·6	21·7
Other right wing groups	87	16·0	14·0
Miscellaneous	—	—	1·4
Overseas deputies (all shades)	83		
	627		

It would be injudicious to say that electoral ingenuity had saved the Fourth Republic: many factors were involved, and it is a complex business to analyse this election even in an arithmetical way, since the pattern of alliances was differently affected by local factors in different areas. But the result was better from the point of view of political stability than could have been expected under the 1946 system; and it was certainly not unrepresentative of French opinion.

After the 1951 election the R.P.F. crumbled to pieces and the Communist Party was involved in embarrassments of a different kind. The axis of influence thus moved a little further from left to right within the centre parties, or at least from the more highly organised parties to those of the older pattern, in which deputies can act without much regard for party discipline, so long as they have strong local backing. As the 1956 election approached, the electoral law again came into question, and there was a serious chance that it would be modified once more, this time in a direction favouring the traditional parties of the Third Republic, by a return to single-member constituencies and the second ballot. There was again a very difficult period of party bargaining about a new electoral law, and it was only a series of accidents which led to premature dissolution and an election under the 1951 law. Experience this time showed that astute managers (like those of the Poujadist movement) had found ingenious ways of turning the provisions of that law to their own advantage. The results have not in practice caused serious political difficulty, but it seems probable that the question of the electoral law will have to be faced again in 1960: in fact, that it may become the habit before an election for the ruling majority to fix the rules under which the election is to take place. This is not, given the conditions of French politics, as 'undemocratic' as it sounds, since a French majority always contains in itself many points of view, and it is impossible for it to take decisions affecting its members' political existence except by elaborate discussion and compromise.

3. *Italy*

The crisis in Italy was sharper, the remedy proposed was more drastic, but little came of it in the end.

Italy had been ruled in the nineteenth century under a relatively narrow franchise and a system of simple plurality voting in single-member constituencies, without second ballot. This was replaced after the first world war by a wide suffrage and a system of P.R. by the method of highest averages. The new system lasted only for two elections: after the second Mussolini took power (legally enough) during a period of party confusion, and passed through the Assembly a law known as the Acerbo law, which provided that in future elections the party obtaining a plurality (not necessarily a clear majority) should receive two-thirds of the seats. Armed with this majority after the election of 1924, Mussolini held no more elections and made no further attempt to govern through the Chamber of Deputies, which was eventually abolished.

After the second world war, Italian constitution-makers had to piece together some sort of democratic regime, with little support or sympathy from the victorious allies. There were then two large parties, a fairly liberal Catholic party, the Christian Democrats, and a Communist Party reckoned to be numerically the strongest outside the U.S.S.R. and China: a number of small anti-Fascist parties: and the remnants of Fascist organisations, which might again coalesce into a movement if conditions favoured them. The first electoral law, passed by the Constituent Assembly in 1948, provided for a simple list system of P.R. An electoral quotient was calculated by dividing votes cast by seats to be filled plus one in constituencies of up to 20 seats, plus two in larger constituencies. There was one single-member constituency, the Val d'Aosta, and thirty multi-member constituencies; and in these thirty constituencies seats were allocated to the parties on the basis of the electoral quotient. 'Remainders' (unused votes) were carried forward from the constituencies to a national pool, for all parties which secured at least one seat in a constituency: and the remaining seats were distributed nationally between parties on the greatest remainder system.

This system favoured the stronger parties somewhat (but not extravagantly): it also favoured party discipline and centralisation, as the law contained only a weak provision for preferential voting. The Chamber elected under it in 1948 contained a majority of Christian Democrats, based on rather less than a majority of the votes cast.

	Seats	Percentage of Total Seats	Percentage of Votes Cast
Christian Democrats	304	53·1	48·5
Other 'democratic' parties	61	10·7	13·4
Communists and allies	183	31·9	31·0
Extreme Right	20	3·4	4·8
Miscellaneous	5	·9	2·3
	573[1]	100·0	100·0

A general election was due in 1953, and in 1951 and 1952 there were signs of a weakening in the position of the Christian Democrats. At local government elections in these years there was not much total gain in Communist strength, but the Communists spread into new areas in the South: the monarchists and neo-fascists gained much more substantially, particularly in the same areas, and the Christian Democrat share of the total vote dropped to 35·5%. It therefore seemed unlikely that there would under the old system of voting be a Christian Democrat majority after the election of 1953; and in the summer of 1952 the government proposed a new scheme, which became law in an amended form after extremely bitter controversy.

From our point of view there were two striking features in the Scelba law (as it became known):—

(a) The system of alliances (already used in Italian local elections) was introduced into national elections.

(b) These were to be national alliances, and it was provided that if a single party or alliances secured (by however small a margin) more than 50% of the votes cast in the whole country it should be given 65% of the seats in the Assembly, 385 out of 590.

[1]Excluding Val d'Aosta.

These two factors were added to the existing system of local constituencies *plus* national pool, and the real complications of the plan were due to this combination. Votes had first to be counted nationally, to discover if any alliance or party was entitled to the premium: if there was to be a premium, there then had to be an arrangement for working out how many seats each party got in each constituency. This meant working out different quotients for different parties, and would have led to queer results, as in some constituencies parties not in the majority would have secured a large majority of seats.

But in fact none of this came into play, because the Christian Democrats and their allies failed by a narrow margin—57,000 votes out of a total of $24\frac{1}{4}$ million—to obtain the necessary quota of 50% plus one vote. (The narrowness of the margin indicated at least great honesty in electoral management.) The effect of the other parts of the system—highest average *plus* exclusion of small parties from the national pool *plus* alliances—was to give a slight advantage to the large parties, Communists as well as Christian Democrats, but the result was a very fair representation of the electoral vote.

	Seats gained	Percentage of total seats	Percentage of total vote
Christian Democrats	262	44·4	40·09
Parties in alliance	38	6·4	9·1
Communists and allies	218	36·9	35·3
Monarchists and neo-Fascists	69	11·8	12·7
Miscellaneous	3	·5	2·81
	590	100·0	100·0

In a sense the system had played a practical joke on its inventors: the Christian Democrats did not secure their majority, their position in the Chamber was precarious, yet Italian politics went on without more turbulence than usual. Indeed, Italy has enjoyed a period of at least relative calm and prosperity: but the Scelba Law remains in the statute book and must be discussed again before the election due in 1958.

4. *Germany*

The position of the German Federal Republic is somewhat different, as it has not been seriously threatened internally by extremes of Right or Left. It has, however, been haunted by the ghosts of the Weimar Republic and of Hitler, and oppressed by the dominance of Communism in Eastern Germany. The moral was drawn from past experience that a stable regime could not be based on a system of representation which encouraged the growth of numerous small parties and cut representatives off from the electors by putting the effective choice of candidates in the hands of the party bureaucracies. This was agreed by almost everyone: British and American advisers, relying on their own experience, went on to preach the necessity for a simple two-party system based on 'first past the post' voting in single-member constituencies. Germans were not convinced by these arguments, probably with good reason, because the two-party system has little basis in German traditions: nevertheless, the American and British models were influential.

In Germany, as in France and Italy, there is still no electoral law that can be regarded as permanent and above party controversy: one law was used for the elections of 1949, a new law for those of 1953, and some further modifications (not of great importance) were made for those of 1957. Some stability therefore seems to be emerging, and it will be enough for our purpose to explain the three main points of the law of 1953.

(a) There are at least 484 seats in the lower house of the Federal Assembly, the *Bundestag*: 242 of these are to be filled by direct election on a simple plurality system in local constituencies, the rest are to be filled proportionately at the national level, by a list system using the method of highest average. Each voter has two votes: he casts one for the candidate whom he favours in his local constituency, the other for the party which he favours at the national level. These votes need not coincide, and need not both be used: but in practice electors generally vote 'the straight ticket'. The results of the constituency elections are settled by simple plurality: the voting on party lists is then consulted, and each party's total of seats is made up from the national list to the total to which it is proportionately entitled. If a party has gained more seats in the local constituencies than it is entitled to have by its share of the national vote (as may happen) it is nevertheless allowed to keep them. The House will generally therefore be a little larger than the minimum figure of 484 (from 1953 to 1957 it had 488 members).

This is an ingenious combination of the 'Anglo-Saxon' preference for single-member constituencies and local affiliations with the continental preference for proportionality and party lists. So far, it appears to have worked as planned.

(b) Formal alliances between parties at the national level are not allowed, but the combination of a multi-party system with single-member constituencies offers considerable advantages to parties which can strike an unofficial bargain. If one party abstains from putting up a candidate at the local level in one constituency (though continuing to compete at national level), it expects its ally to do as much for it somewhere else: the single-member system thus produces something of its natural effect of consolidation of blocs.

(c) The system has built into it a considerable bias against smaller parties. The system used at the national level is that of the highest average, and in addition no party is admitted to consideration at this level unless it either secures 50% of the total list votes cast, or wins at least one local seat. An exception is made in favour of parties representing localised minorities, which need gain 50% only in their own area: but no party has been successful in this way. The effect of this provision has been to reduce the number of parties represented to six, and three of these have only 46 seats between them out of 488. There are three other parties which would have secured a few seats (not more than 16 together) but for the restriction on smaller parties: one of these is the Communist Party, which obtained only 2·2% of the total list vote, and in spite of great efforts was not successful in winning the one local seat on which it had concentrated its strength. Apart from this deliberate attack on minor parties, the relation between seats and votes is close.

(d) There are relatively strict provisions for regulating the internal affairs of parties, by insisting that the nomination of candidates is to be accompanied by a properly certified record of the procedure by which they were nominated, including a secret ballot of those entitled to vote. It has in fact become the practice that there should be open contests within parties for nomination, almost comparable to American primaries. There are also provisions that parties must have a properly elected executive committee, a party statute and a programme: but parties which had appreciable representation in 1953 are exempt from formal regulation, so that these provisions are hortatory rather than effective.

This system is the most elaborate piece of electoral engineering yet tried. One of its tendencies is to strengthen the position of the two biggest parties, the Christian Democrats and the Social Democrats: but for this the law could not have been passed. The system is, however, also designed to encourage certain lines of development in German political life, and to discourage others. Such devices often have unexpected effects, and the system has not yet been exposed to a period of great strain. Nevertheless, it has worked as planned, so far.

5. *The Ethical Problem*

The ethical case against these experiments in political engineering is that they use undemocratic methods in order to defend democracy, they do evil that good may come. They 'do evil' in the sense that although they accept universal suffrage as the basis of the state, they do not follow consistently the logic (or any of the alternative forms of logic) of the electoral process in converting votes cast by the electorate into power in the elected assembly. A system is contrived which partially disfranchises those who vote for certain parties: to this extent the system is not a free and equal one. Indeed, it justifies itself only by setting alongside the argument for democracy another argument, that for the maintenance of the state through the effective power of those who control it; and to this extent it concedes the Fascist or Marxist argument that the state is not the expression of the consent of all its citizens, but an instrument of control in the hands of those who possess power.

An answer must take the line that one-sided arguments are out of place in politics; absolute purity of democratic logic is impossible because it would destroy democracy, and there can be no obligation upon leaders to follow logic to the destruction of themselves, their followers, and their cause. Certain things are good; one of them is freedom in elections. Certain things are bad: one of these is government by repression, which refuses to acknowledge that popular consent has a place in politics. It is a duty to seek what is good and to avoid what is bad; not to sacrifice what is partly good because it is also partly bad. Half a loaf is better than no bread: it is also better than a quarter of a loaf, because it gives more strength and confidence to work for three-quarters of a loaf tomorrow, a whole loaf in the end. But this view of politics goes on to assert that the whole loaf can never be attained by weak and fallible men—improvement is possible, but not perfection, in politics or in any other human activity. It is possible, further, to turn perfectionist logic against the perfectionists by showing that there is no practicable system of voting, however simple and clear at first sight, which does not upon inspection reveal logical flaws of its own; and that an attempt to introduce logically perfect voting systems is as likely to lead to the creation and defence of vested interests as is the electoral engineering of the 1950s.

It will be obvious that the author's sympathies lie on this side of the argument: but it must be recognised that there are dangers inherent in the practice of ingenious compromise. It is true that it is the intention of the parties to move towards greater equality in voting when it is safe to do so, and certain forces tell in that direction, because the alliance of centre parties tends to relax as soon as pressure is withdrawn, and they may then bid against one another in seeking new support by liberalising the system. But this process of change is likely to be intricate and slow, since many interests are involved: the system creates such interests, and in so far as it secures stability it is also likely to be successful in perpetuating itself.

It must be remembered too that excessive ingenuity tends to defeat the practical aims of free elections referred to in Chapter I. It does not give the country as a whole a feeling that it is brought into consultation by the government, since a section of the electorate is systematically and deliberately unrepresented, and people know that they will be under-represented so long as they continue to vote in a particular way. Similarly, too much ingenuity may fail to smooth the process by which one government succeeds another: the process may be easy within the ring of centre parties which constitute the regime, but there can be no move outside this circle except by violent change. Finally, there is the risk that tinkering with electoral law may become a habit: no electorate can have much faith in a system which is reconstructed before each election by the majority in power.

The matter can be summed up by looking back to the criteria set out in Chapter VIII. All these systems give priority to the third criterion, that of securing a collectively effective assembly: the other criteria are not disregarded, but they are rated much lower than is usual in the other countries where elections are free. Further advance along this line might lead to the notion of one-party democracy, to elections which are elections only in name, because everything in them is subordinated to the need to maintain the existing regime in power. It is obvious that in 'doctored' systems everything is not thus subordinated; other criteria do play an important part. Furthermore, these systems play fair according to their own rules. There are 'jokers' in the system, but the elections are properly conducted, with complete freedom of debate, absence of direct corruption or intimidation, and extreme scrupulousness in voting procedure and in counting the votes. The next two parts of this book emphasise how important these things are: if this basis is sound free elections are possible, without it they are unthinkable. This combination of scrupulousness and ingenuity is not a bad foundation for a free and stable political order: but one cannot speak of success till the fabric has been created and has acquired a patina of traditional loyalty.

Part Three: Administration and Adjudication

CHAPTER XI

Methods of Management

1. *Introductory*

Politicians debating the construction of electoral systems talk mainly about the matters set out in Parts One and Two of this book. But this is not more than half the story. Decisions about the qualifications of voters and candidates and about forms of voting directly affect the character of an electoral system: democracy is sometimes measured by the slogans 'one man one vote', 'one vote one value'—everyone to count for one, and none for more than one. But any system, however democratic its form may be in this sense, can be twisted in operation so that it becomes something quite different. To put the same thing in another way, an electoral system comprehends much more than the formal questions so far discussed. Three further conditions must be fulfilled, each of them with wide implications. There must be an administrative system efficient enough to conduct an election without confusion, inaccuracy and bickering over trifles. There must be some means of ensuring that adjudication on the merits of cases arising under the electoral law is outside the hands of the government of the day, because there is always suspicion that the government is seeking to 'make' the elections in its own favour. There must be a code of political *mores* embodied in law and practice, which sets bounds to the bitterness of the contest for power: and such a code must have sanctions enforceable against those who break it, enforceable by the combined strength of public opinion and independent judical decision.

It will be clear that in these three ways the electoral system is tied in to other parts of the political system. Free elections will not work unless there is a competent civil service, a judicial power independent of the government in office and trusted to adjudicate without fear or favour, and a strong public opinion capable of checking a drift towards violence and corruption. Part Four deals with this question of electoral morality. In Part Three we are concerned with problems relating primarily to the machinery for administration and adjudication.

These problems can be solved only by efficient and independent bodies of administrators and judges, and it may be convenient to begin by sketching the available answers to the practical questions: who is to run the election? who is to adjudicate in matters of dispute? No system, however elegant, will command public confidence if it is administered by men under the direct orders of the government of the day, and if these men have full power to decide all disputed questions of law and fact. Indeed there are few governments anywhere which would in such circumstances resist the temptation to 'make' the election in their own interest. There was in the nineteenth century an established tradition in Europe, particularly in France, of elections 'made' by the government through its henchmen, the prefects or provincial governors. This is in a sense no more than the equivalent of electoral engineering: freedom is allowed, up to a point, but it is doled out sparingly, lest it endanger the stability of the regime and of the government in power, which takes the precaution of retaining some extra aces in its own hands. But the 'twist' in the 'engineered' systems of the 1950s is there in the law for all to see: the 'twist' in 'made' elections is more insidious because more hypocritical—no one can measure its limits. It is therefore a cause for relief that in Western countries electoral administration and adjudication (though not perfect) are almost everywhere outside the direct control of governments. The 'making' of elections is now an art practised mainly in the Middle East and in Latin America, where public morality is low and the civil service and judiciary are not strong and independent powers within the state. It remains to be seen how matters will go in the new states which are emerging from the old colonial empires.

There are three elements out of which an independent system of electoral administration and adjudication can be made: the elected assembly itself: the civil service: the judiciary. It is possible out of these elements, jointly or separately, to construct the nucleus of a separate and continuous organisation for the conduct of elections; but it must be remembered that elections (even if one includes all elections, local as well as central) are things that come in waves, bringing sudden crises of enormously heavy work, and that in a system in which the assembly can be dissolved at short notice the timing of these crises is not wholly predictable. It is therefore impossible to keep a fully staffed electoral 'service' or 'commission' continuously in being. The nucleus of such a body may be continuous, but in times of general election it is dependent on very large reinforcements from some other source.

2. *The elected assembly*

There is a tradition that the independence of an elected assembly requires that the assembly itself should have exclusive power to decide controversies about its membership. It may even be asserted, in extreme cases, that this power ought to over-ride the ordinary law enforced through the courts, and there have in British history been a number of unresolved conflicts of this kind between the House of Commons and the courts of law, which are (at least in form) *royal* courts, the King's (or Queen's) courts, not Parliament's courts. The courts never admitted that the House had the right to make general rules about membership and about elections, but until 1868 it was settled law that only the House could decide specific cases about corrupt or illegal practices during parliamentary elections; the House could decide which of the claimants was entitled to a disputed seat, and could punish a corrupt electorate by disfranchising the constituency. The House acted through committees, but the final decision in each case depended on a vote of the whole House; evidence was heard by the committees, and some respect was paid to the decencies of judicial procedure, but most decisions were in the end taken (often after tacit bargaining) on political grounds. This rather sordid haggling became in the end an embarrassment to the House itself, and in 1868 it transferred its responsibility for adjudication to an 'election court' consisting of two judges of the High Court, in England and Wales and in Ireland, and of the Court of Session in Scotland. The judges were at that time reluctant to assume an invidious responsibility, but the transfer was one of several factors which led to a decline in the number of disputed cases, and electoral petitions are now very rare indeed.

The older tradition is maintained in the French National Assembly (as well as in certain other elected bodies in France) which begins its life by appointing committees for *vérification de pouvoirs*, whose business it is to certify that each member has been properly elected and is entitled to act. The committees 'save' an important point of French constitution in principle, which forbids the judiciary to interfere in settling the composition of the legislature: but their proceedings are not much more reputable than were those of House of Commons committees in the eighteenth and early nineteenth centuries. There are some instances elsewhere of countries which maintain in this way the principle of 'separation of powers' and do not suffer the same political embarrassment: and it would be possible for the elected house to delegate responsibility for managing its elections and for adjudicating about them to an independent body set up by resolution of the house itself, and not by law, thus 'saving' the principle involved. But such arrangements are bound to throw some strain on political morality and on public confidence, because they make a majority within a body of elected persons judge in its own cause; and there is little doubt that it is better to let the separation of powers go, and to use fully the resources of the administration and the judiciary. The practical justification of the old practice was that it began when both administration and judiciary (in so far as they existed effectively at all) were instruments of royal power, and an elected body dared not put itself in the hands of people whom it was (at least in part) elected to oppose.

3. *The administration*

Probably officials of the executive can never be wholly independent of the government in power. To say that it is 'in power' means primarily that it has legal authority to direct the work of officials. There are, however, four ways in which some independence can be secured, the first perhaps of theoretical importance only.

(a) *An election government.* There was in the constitution of the Fourth Republic in France, until amended in 1954, a provision that in the event of dissolution of the Assembly by a government in power the Prime Minister and the Minister of the Interior should lose their posts; the former was to be replaced by the President of the Assembly, who would appoint a new Minister of the Interior with the consent of the (all-party) *bureau* of the Assembly, and would also bring into the government one member of each group in the Assembly not already represented in the government. No government was likely to risk dissolution on these terms, and there was no dissolution in the period up to 1954, when the rule was altered so as to permit the government to remain in office unchanged. It is unlikely that such a system could really work in practice anywhere.

(b) *A non-political civil service.* The administration, or some parts of it, has in some countries acquired by law or tradition quite substantial independence, so that it is trusted not to accept directives from political superiors except in so far as these are given officially and in proper legal form. In Britain the supervision of electoral machinery is in the hands of a small division of the Home Office, which advises the government about technical matters of procedure in elections, and issues circulars and instructions to subordinate authorities. These are considerable powers, but there is an established tradition that the administrative class of the Civil Service in Britain is 'non-political', and this tradition is strong enough to influence attitudes about the division which deals with elections, a tiny part of the whole service and wholly committed to its tradition. The Home Office in these matters is above suspicion: the French Ministry of the Interior is not, and it may be thought guilty even when it is innocent, because there is a long tradition that the Minister of the Interior and his prefects are the men who 'make' the election for the government in power.

The position is further compromised in France because there has always been a direct line of responsibility from the Minister through the prefects to sub-prefects and mayors. In Britain, on the other hand, there are peculiar and rather archaic forms of independence in the administration at lower levels. Registration is in the hands of County Clerks and Town Clerks, who are servants not of the central government but of autonomous local authorities, and are strongly marked by the traditions of their own profession. As Registration Officers, they act independently in execution of statutory duties, and are paid by fees separate from their salaries: no one thinks of them as servants of the government in power. There is a separate office of Returning Officer, filled by different office-holders in different constituencies: Sheriffs, Under-Sheriffs, Mayors of Boroughs, Chairmen of Urban District Councils. These office-holders are all persons standing by tradition outside party politics: some of them are merely titular functionaries with no substantial duties, all leave their electoral duties in the hands of an organisation provided by the Clerk's department of the local authority concerned. It is unlikely that such historical curiosities of this sort are to be found elsewhere: the general point which emerges is that it is useful to employ in electoral management outlying and semi-independent officials, who are not (and are not thought to be) closely associated with the government in office.

(c) *Division of responsibility*. The third point arises out of this British example. One quite effective safeguard in such matters is that of diffusion of power among different authorities. Responsibility for managing British elections is scattered between the Electoral Boundary Commission, the Registration Officers, the Returning Officers, and a number of judicial authorities, loosely coordinated by a few administrative civil servants in the Home Office. It is both a weakness and an advantage of such a system that very few people understand fully how it works: it is an undoubted advantage that any attempt at improper action by an official somewhere in the system would be challenged at once by some other official independent of him. This sort of system is not easy to imitate or to create artificially, but it suggests that this is not a matter in which it is desirable to seek administrative tidiness at all costs.

(d) *A special authority for elections*. A much neater arrangement is to provide by law that for specified purposes connected with elections specified officials are to take their orders solely from an independent electoral commission. This works satisfactorily if there is general confidence in the commission, and if the public are prepared to believe that officials dependent on their usual superiors for advancement in their careers will during the period of elections follow strictly the orders of other masters, and will disregard suggestions put to them improperly by politicians through the ordinary channels of administration. This ought to be possible, in a well-constituted bureaucracy, when promotion is properly regulated: but it represents a fairly high level of administrative development, and the public are not always ready to believe in it even where it exists.

4. *The judiciary*

Here everything depends on the existing status of the judiciary and of the opinion which supports it. This is at its strongest where the judges are at the apex of an organised legal profession, a great 'interest' in the state, led by able and independent men, and seen by the public to stand for the ideas of impartial procedure and of the 'rule of law'. If this tradition exists, there are perhaps three ways in which it can be used.

(a) *The ordinary courts.* All matters of adjudication can be put into the hands of the judges of the ordinary courts, sitting either in their usual capacity or as 'election judges' specially nominated under the electoral laws. This is the strongest way of bringing judicial prestige to bear on the conduct of elections.

(b) *'Revising barristers.'* In hotly contested elections there may be more business to do than the ordinary judges can handle with reasonable care within a reasonable time. A familiar British example of this relates to the process of registration, which gave rise at first to endless disputes between parties about the entitlement of individual voters. The problem of adjudication was solved by appointing for this purpose many numerous temporary subordinate judges, the 'revising barristers', who dealt judicially (they exist now only in Northern Ireland) with disputes about registration. This arrangement was possible only because of the existence of a legal profession large enough to supply on short notice reasonably effective judges not associated with either side in a local quarrel. There will, of course, be an additional safeguard if appeals lie from temporary judges to the ordinary courts, or to a special election court.

The special value of a system of this kind is that it extends the judicial power widely enough for it to play a substantial part in the working of an election. An attempt at more elaborate legal procedure would probably mean more, not less, administrative power, because the delay and expense involved would discourage reference to courts of law.

(c) *'Judicialised' administration.* Finally, a judicial person may as electoral commissioner be put in charge of all arrangements for an election: or an electoral commissioner appointed from outside the judiciary may be given a tenure of appointment similar to that of a judge, so that he becomes a sort of extra judge, of a rather special kind. The line which divides judicial from administrative duties is so narrow that there is not much theoretical objection to this, and where the judiciary has great prestige it may be justifiable to use it in this particularly delicate kind of administration. But there is always the risk that to involve the judiciary directly in the management of elections may drag it into party politics and weaken general confidence in its impartiality.

5. *Electoral Commissions*

There is no particular magic in the fashionable title of 'Electoral Commissioner'. Its meaning depends entirely on the degree of independence given to the Commission and the scope of its responsibilities. Besides, an Electoral Commission cannot enlist a complete electoral 'service' of its own to work for it, and it is therefore in the last resort dependent on ordinary officials temporarily placed at its disposal.

(a) *Degree of independence.* This is naturally a matter of gradations. At one extreme are bodies sponsored from outside the political system concerned: for example the special body, set up by international agreement and consisting of an Indian (in the chair), an American, an Englishman, an Egyptian and three Sudanese, which managed the elections leading to independence in the Sudan: or such bodies as the U.N.O. commission which was responsible for plebiscites about the future of the section of Togoland under British administration. The closest parallel to such external bodies that can be reached within the system is to constitute a panel of judges to act as Electoral Commissioners of a special kind, or to give the Electoral Commissioner judicial tenure of office and to surround him with the traditional appurtenances of a judge, as is done in India. Below this level, there are various gradations and alternatives. There may be a commission of administrators, with a special statutory basis; there may be a mixed commission of elder statesmen, judges and administrators: in Britain the Speaker of the House of Commons, an independent person of great dignity, is used as chairman of the Electoral Boundary Commission. Finally, at the opposing extreme is the purely administrative device (used for instance for African elections in Kenya) of handing over to one senior official within the administration responsibility for the business of managing the election, acting through the usual channels of the administrative organisation. This last device may be of great value administratively, but it has little bearing in the question of political impartiality and public confidence.

(b) *Scope of responsibility.* There are three lines of division here:

(i) The Commission may or may not be given responsibility for all the administrative business of the election: for instance in Britain there is a commission which deals only with the vexed question of constituency boundaries.

(ii) The Commission may be administrative only, and an appeal may lie from its decisions to a court of law: or it may (perhaps with some internal separation of function) be responsible both for ordinary administration and for deciding disputed cases.

(iii) The Commission may have absolutely final power of decision; or there may be an appeal from it to the courts; or there may be a reserve power to override it in the hands of the government and the assembly, acting either together or separately.

This description of possible permutations is perhaps tedious, but they deserve emphasis. A great variety of administrative and judicial tools are available for the management of elections; the combination to be chosen in particular circumstances depends on the political resources available in a given situation, and there is no overriding consideration except that elections cannot be considered free if management and adjudication are wholly controlled by the government of the day.

CHAPTER XII

Delimitation of Constituencies

1. *Introductory*

Perhaps it has not in earlier chapters been stressed sufficiently that all elections to numerous assemblies take place through territorial constituencies. This need not be true of elections like the American presidential election, nor of plebiscites and referenda, though delimitation may be important in these instances: and there are, of course, borderline cases— in some countries some local councils with as many as fifteen or twenty members are chosen by the electorate as a whole. There are even exceptions to prove rules, such as the election of the Parliament of Israel, 120 members, in a single block. But no one now would dream of accepting J. S. Mill's notion that a single assembly of about 600 members could be elected by all the electors voting in a single constituency. There is an approximation to J. S. Mill's ideal in these systems which carry forward 'unused' votes from local constituencies to regional and national pools; but even these systems must be based on territorial delimitation of the original constituencies.

Such delimitation is always, even in these cases, of considerable political importance. It is important in two ways. First, the way in which boundaries are drawn affects the general character of the assembly, because it decides the sort of units on which members depend for election and which they are supposed to 'represent'. Secondly, delimitation (or 'districting', as it is called in the U.S.A.) may also affect the fortunes of individuals and of political parties, because the distribution of votes between constituencies influences their effectiveness. The extreme case is that of the practice of 'gerrymandering' single-member constituencies, so as deliberately to give greater value to the votes of one party than to those of another; but no system of P.R. has been (or can be) devised in which the political fate of individuals is not to some extent affected by the way in which boundary lines are drawn on an electoral map.

The arguments about these two problems interlock: as in debate about electoral qualifications and about voting systems, arguments of a general and philosophical kind are invoked to justify solutions which help one party or another. But a workable distinction can be drawn between general criteria on the one hand, tactical devices and their control on the other.

2. *General criteria*

The general arguments are in principle simple enough. A balance has to be drawn between (on the one hand) equality of districts, on the other hand administrative convenience and localised political interests.

'Equal electoral districts' formed part of the programme of radical reform in England in the 1830s, the only part of that programme which has not been realised. The slogan represented an attack on a system in which (even after the Reform Act of 1832) the difference between the smallest and the largest constituencies electing the same number of members was of the order of 1 : 60, a difference which entailed a corresponding difference in the 'value' of a vote. In the course of electoral reform the old principle that members should represent corporate units of government, shires and boroughs, disappeared, and by the 1880s the new principle of representation on the basis of special electoral districts or constituencies was generally accepted. But even after the redistribution of seats in 1885 the range of difference between constituencies, in terms of numbers of qualified electors, was of the order of 1 : 7. There has been much further redistribution of seats since the 1880s, and the idea of equal electoral districts is now admitted to be a guiding principle. But even after a thorough reorganisation of constituencies in 1948 the range of size among normal constituencies was of the order of 1 : 2, if a few unusual constituencies are included it was 1 : 3. It is obvious that the principle of equality had met certain obstacles; it is likely that these obstacles are a lasting part of the political system in Britain, and that they are present in some form in all systems of single-member constituencies.

There are perhaps four main arguments which tell against equality:

(a) *Community of local interest.* It is no longer true that members of an assembly are sent there solely by a local community to represent it; members represent also (on the one hand) a large number of individual voters who expect their member to help them as individuals, on the other hand non-territorial interests grouped in political parties and in other organisations which have some basis other than locality. But in most countries local feeling is alive: in some it is still very strong, and is backed by a 'locality rule' governing the qualifications of candidates (p. 39 above). It may often prove impossible to divide a district which has strong common interests which it seeks to press in the assembly through its member or members; or to unite in a single district communities whose interests conflict. British electoral law contains a schedule of factors to be taken into account by the Electoral Boundary Commissioners in deliminating constituencies. They require that 'so far as is practicable' no major local authority is to be linked with another major authority to form one constituency, and no minor authority is to be divided between two constituencies: but the Commissioners may break these rules in order to avoid 'excessive disparity' between the electorate of any constituency and the average or 'quota', and to take account of 'special geographical considerations, in particular the size, shape, and accessibility of a constituency'. 'Excessive disparity' and 'special geographical considerations' are intangible and imponderable factors: they cannot be measured objectively by any independent body, and the balance between them and the factor of local interest is judged only by the volume of protest aroused by particular decisions.

(b) *Administrative convenience.* Unity of administrative area is relevant partly because it reflects (and perhaps creates) community of interest: but the same criterion is important for convenience in managing the election. Elections must in general be run by officials engaged also on other administrative business, and it adds to their difficulties if electoral boundaries cut across the boundaries to which they are accustomed. If this happens, everything has to be constructed afresh for this single purpose—chain of command, channels of communication, registers, statistics—and in the process there can be much loss of time and efficiency. It therefore helps administrators if the smallest ordinary administrative districts are used as bricks out of which to build constituencies.

(c) *'Geographical considerations'.* No attempt has been made in this book to deal with the complex of arguments about the proper conduct of an elected member, as this would take us into rather a different sphere of debate: among much disagreement it would probably be agreed on all hands that it is in some sense the member's business to be in contact with his constituents. This can be interpreted in different ways, but however it is taken it is obvious that in a diversified country, if all districts have approximately the same number of voters, some members will find 'contact' more difficult than do others, because of relatively bad communications and scattered population. It is therefore usual to allow large, sparsely-populated districts a rather more generous allocation of seats than that to which they are numerically entitled. British electoral law contains a direction to this effect, and there are a few constituencies, such as the Western Islands and Orkney and Shetland, which have a roll of voters much below the average.

(d) *The timing of redistribution.* Finally, there are difficulties caused by the passage of time. In the modern world movements of population may upset an equal delimitation of constituencies in a comparatively short time. In about twenty-five years, from 1918 to 1944, the range of size of normal constituencies in Great Britain grew from about 1 : 3 to about 1 : 12; at the 1945 election—if special arrangements had not been made—the smallest single-members constituency of the ordinary type would have had about 15,000 voters, the largest about 200,000. This was the result of the decline of old industrial areas, the growth of new ones, and the bombing of the hearts of the great cities. There may be substantial changes even in a shorter period; but a piecemeal readjustment of boundaries is not easy, because constituencies interlock like pieces of a puzzle and the search for equality may require a general re-shuffle of the electoral map. Such re-shuffling has many inconveniences. It means that a great many politicians must sort themselves out among new constituencies, that the machinery of party organisation and electoral administration has to be reconstructed, that electors are grouped in different ways, and that the local adherents of the parties find themselves on different committees meeting with different people in different places. All these difficulties can be overcome, but only with some sacrifice of political solidarity and continuity.

3. *Gerrymandering, honest and otherwise*

In the last section a simple argument about equality confronted a number of arguments of a more complex kind, in which practical considerations were mixed up with notions about the nature of representation and the functions of a representative. Gerrymandering (which might be defined as adjusting electoral boundaries so as to secure some object besides equal representation) is not often barefaced. Even when it is carried out in the interests of a party in power, that party generally finds arguments to show that it is acting in accordance with principle: and sometimes the manipulation of boundaries can be an effective instrument in such good causes as the protection of minorities and the maintenance of local traditions.

For obvious reasons, such manipulation is much more important with single-member constituencies than with large districts, with 'first past the post' voting than with any form of proportional representation: the reduction of the difficulties sketched in this chapter is one of the arguments in favour of list systems with national pools.

Little need be said of manipulation carried out simply to increase the share of seats secured by the party in power. It is obvious how this can be done: and a glance at the shapes of the electoral districts shown in the U.S. *Congressional Directory* suggests that there are at least some American states in which nineteenth-century traditions die hard. The interesting cases are those in which good reasons are given for manipulation. There are four familiar examples:—

(a) *Rural virtues.* There is an old doctrine that the country is entitled to better representation than the towns simply because it is the country, the seat of all political virtue, the touchstone of patriotism. This may be done frankly and constitutionally: until 1952 the Norwegian constitution contained a specific guarantee that the country districts regardless of population should be entitled to twice as many seats as all the towns together: New Zealand had a similar rule, in the electoral law but not in the constitution, until 1946. This represented a sort of tradition that there is a separate 'estate' of farmers or peasants, whose prosperity is essential to the country: it also represented a political balance, now passing away, in which the farmers could decide the day between city parties.

The same arguments can be used to justify the systematic over-representation of farmers and small towns in State legislatures and in the Federal House of Representatives in the U.S.A. Here there is no constitutional or statutory defence of the system, except the provision that the making of electoral districts is a matter for the States and not for the Union; in many States the balance of power is such that the old system perpetuates itself. In other countries regimes dependent on the rural vote can increase the relative strength of their supporters without going the length of open arguments for inequality. If seats are allocated on the basis of population, not of registered electors, this generally favours the country, as the proportion of children is usually higher there. Local government areas are generally less populous in the country than in the towns, and therefore a system of delimitation that pays special attention to the unity of administrative areas is likely to have a bias in favour of the countryside, even though it also seeks equality. A result of one sort follows if towns are picked out of the countryside as separate constituencies, even perhaps to the extent of making a 'district of burghs' into a single urban constituency, as was done in several instances in Scotland in the nineteenth century: the electoral results may well be different if towns are merged with country-side, or if their suburbs are split off and linked with rural constituencies.

In Western countries the argument generally favours country against town, in Australia, Canada, South Africa, and for the French second chamber, as well as in the examples already given. It is perhaps worth mentioning that for Marxists there are grounds for using similar reason-ing in reverse. The early forms of Soviet government in Russia under-represented the peasants, and in Yugoslavia at one time towns were linked with country (not for parliamentary purposes, but in local government councils) to strengthen the influence of the townsman against the farmer.

(b) *Built-in bias.* It is not generally noticed that unless there is propor-tional representation with fairly large constituencies or with a national pool even perfect equality in the delimitation of constituencies may involve a bias in favour of one party or another. The simplest case is that of Britain, where Labour party voters are on the whole more concentrated geographically than are Conservative voters. In con-sequence, Labour wins more seats by large majorities than do the

Conservatives: of 35 majorities over 20,000 votes in the 1955 elections, 22 were on the side of Labour. The cumulative effect of this over the whole country is that there is a 'bias' in the system of about 2% against Labour; the parties would be equal in the House of Commons if Labour got 51% of the votes cast for the two parties, the Conservatives 49%.

In this situation equality could be restored only by deliberate gerrymandering. This is now out of the question in Britain, but the argument is available for use elsewhere. It is easy to defend disparities in the size of constituencies so long as there is no great disparity in the ratio between seats and votes as between the main parties.

(c) *Minority representation.* Reference was made in Chapter IV to the difficulty of giving any guarantee of minority representation in a multiracial society except by introducing communal electorates. So long as the minority is geographically coherent the problem is not in practice as difficult as it looks; there is no risk of Welsh under-representation in the British Parliament. Where the position is a little less precise, a good deal can be done by an agreed instruction to those responsible for constituency boundaries, that they are to produce the result that in at least "x" constituencies the minority to be protected is in the majority. This possibility was recognised in Ceylon by the Donoughmore Commission which reported in 1928: at the time of writing (1957) a commission has been instructed to try to find a similar solution in Mauritius.

(d) *Protection of local interests.* The last paragraph perhaps deals with a special case of a more general problem, that of ascertaining 'real' communities and giving them a chance to be heard. A town which has 'its' member of parliament is psychologically in a stronger position, it 'feels better', than one which is merged in a larger constituency or divided between two constituencies; and in Britain it is of some political importance that each big city has 'its' members, who act together for some local purpose regardless of party. Delimitation based simply on equality tells against this sort of political sentiment, because boundaries which are fair numerically are certain to cut through local interests and communities. Where (as in Britain) those defining constituencies are instructed to give weight to local sentiment—and the practical reason for this is that loud protests are heard if they do not—they are thereby encouraged to increase inequalities of number in the distribution of seats; and the process can of course be carried much further, much less honestly.

4. *The mechanics of redistribution.*

It is tempting to ask why political parties cannot agree to appoint a judicial body to settle electoral districts, give it agreed instructions and then leave it alone. Some of the difficulties have been seen in Britain in our experience of the work of the Electoral Boundary Commissions, set up for the first time in 1944. There are four of these bodies, the Commissioners for England, for Wales, for Scotland and for Northern Ireland. The Speaker of the House of Commons is titular chairman of all of them, and all also include the appropriate Registrar-General, an authority on surveying, and two other officials, appointed by the Ministers concerned but completely outside party politics. The terms of reference of the Commissions, as they now stand, were summarised on p. 108 above: the Commissions may make reports at any time, must survey the situation in the whole country at intervals of not less than three or more than seven years.

The Commissions were set up in order to 'take redistribution out of politics': it had been a matter of politics for over a hundred years, and the results had satisfied no one. But in practice the importance of the subject in a single-member, 'first past the post' system made it impossible for the government to abdicate responsibility, even by agreement between the parties. The Commissions do not decide; they enquire, hold hearings and recommend. The Cabinet decides what proposals to lay before Parliament in the form of a draft Order in Council, which requires the assent of both Houses before it is formally made; that is to say, the decision depends ultimately on voting on party lines.

The Cabinet's responsibility has proved to be a real one. Much of the Commissions' work has been accepted without challenge, but it has provoked controversies of two sorts. One was over its original terms of reference, which laid greater stress on equality than does the present formula: the first proposals of the Commissions caused so much protest about the range of size among borough constituencies and about the division of local government areas that the formula was revised, and the Commission tried again, in such a way that the margin between the smallest and largest normal constituencies was increased from about 3 : 5 to 1 : 2. This brought new protests from the now 'under-represented': the government responded by adding a few more seats to the House for distribution by the Commissioners to deserving cases: there followed protests again, because the extra seats were likely (it was said) to go mainly to the Government's party.

The other difficulty is over timing. The Commissions are in effect invited to review the whole situation after each general election and before the next. Movements of population in five years can be quite important: but to take account of them the Commissions may have to disturb a good many constituencies, because the whole pattern interlocks. Hence protests about the dislocation of party organisation and local continuity: the same results have followed in an even more acute form in New Zealand, where elections are held every three years, and a Commission revises constituencies after every quinquennial census. But if revision is not done steadily and regularly a back-log of disparities accumulates: revision becomes an even larger task, and may cause an upheaval which has a marked effect on the relative strength of the parties.

Members of elected assemblies are naturally sensitive to any threat to their own seats through redistribution, and controversies about it become charged with so much personal feeling that the government in power cannot evade responsibility. There is perhaps less difficulty under proportional representation with fairly large constituencies, and delimitation may in such cases come to be regarded mainly as a matter of administration. Where there are single-member constituencies the government often attempts to avoid an embarrassing responsibility by passing the initiative to an independent delimitation commission. But (so far as the author knows) the commission's decisions are nowhere final in law, except in New Zealand, and British experience is typical. A most earnest effort has been made here to 'judicialise' delimitations; the result is a great improvement on the confusion which existed before, but the new system does not (and cannot) avoid embarrassment completely.

CHAPTER XIII

The Register

1. *Introductory*

A good register is the foundation of electoral administration; on this everything rests. The invention of the register was one of these pieces of ingenuity which make advances in the art of government possible, as advances in the technology of measurement make scientific progress possible; and (as happens in such cases) it did not attract much attention at the time. Traditional elections of the 'Anglo-Saxon' type were conducted without registers, and this was one reason for confusion and corruption in handling even the relatively small electorates of that time. The French electoral systems of the revolution and of the Napoleonic period, though more democratic in theory than in practice, had the advantage of resting on an organised administrative system, and permanent electoral lists have existed in France since 1791. The introduction of electoral registers in Britain was one of the decisive steps taken by the Reform Act of 1832, and the necessity of 'attending to the register' became the basis of party organisation in the new constituencies. The system did not at first work well, but its necessity has never been questioned. In a developed system of free elections the process of registration works so smoothly that its importance is scarcely noticed.

2. *Why a register is necessary*

An electoral register consists of an official list of those entitled to vote in the election to which it relates; it specifies the constituencies in which they are to vote, and any other relevant points, for instance, entitlement to postal voting or proxy voting. There are three reasons why a register is essential in a seriously contested election with a large electorate:—

(a) *Adjudication.* It is essential that adjudication on the qualifications of individual electors should be kept separate from the process of voting, and should so far as possible be disposed of in advance. In English elections before the time of registers those claiming to vote presented themselves at the hustings while the poll was open. Most electorates were fairly small, records of previous polls were available, and voters were known personally, so that large scale attempts to claim votes falsely were unlikely. Even so, there were often many disputed votes, and the decision of an election might be delayed by claims and counter-

115

claims long after the end of the poll. With a proper system of registration all this is avoided: the register is compiled, authenticated (by judicial decision if necessary), and closed some time before the poll, and in the polling station the person claiming to vote is expected only to identify himself as a person in the register. Qualifications entitle a man or woman to be placed on the register: a place on the register entitles a man or woman to vote, and those not registered cannot vote.

(b) *Allocation to constituencies.* Chapter XII has emphasised the importance of the division of voters between constituencies, especially in single-member plurality systems. A voter is entitled to vote not in general, but in a particular constituency: the register is a constituency register. If this local allocation were not settled in advance it would be impossible to fight a closely contested election without immense turmoil, as the parties could switch their forces of voters from one constituency to another on polling day.

(c) *Party management.* A register serves also as the basis of organisation in the electoral campaign between parties. When electorates were relatively small and qualifications were of a kind likely to cause dispute, it was an important part of the business of party managers to see that as many as possible of their own supporters were put on the register, and that no supporter of the opposing party was left unchallenged if there was any legal doubt about his claim. This could be a laborious and expensive business. Under universal adult suffrage the exact composition of the register is of much less importance to party managers, except for such matters as entitlement to postal voting or proxy voting, but they still find it useful because it is the only authoritative list of the electors whom they are seeking to convince. A party campaigning with real thoroughness attempts to keep marked copies of the register, divided on the basis of canvassing and personal knowledge into friendly, hostile and doubtful voters: if the election is closely contested this is the basis of a plan for converting doubtful voters and ensuring that faithful voters are brought to the poll.

It is not therefore possible to dispense with a register unless there already exists some other official list which can fulfil the same function. This is not inconceivable: for instance, if the right to vote in a particular area is based on the payment within that area of a specified tax, such as local rates, the register of ratepayers can be used as a register of electors, and the same thing might be done if the franchise were based on occupation of property and there existed an official list of householders. But these cases are exceptional: they cannot occur under universal suffrage, and in any case they do not provide (unless some special arrangement is made) for details such as the specification of postal and proxy voters.

3. *The administrative problem*

The experience of officials in compiling registers is not one of the aspects of democracy about which much has been written, and it is necessary to state the case here partly in general terms and partly in relation to British practice, with limited reference to other systems. But as a matter of deduction from first principles it is clear that there are a number of problems which must be faced under all systems.

(a) *The authority in charge.* It is here necessary only to refer back to what has been said in Chapter XI about the solutions theoretically possible. The practical problem is that of combining incompatible requirements. The job of registration is bound to have large seasonal peaks, however carefully it is planned, and it is therefore best given to someone who has at his disposal a large body of trained clerks who can be transferred temporarily to this work when required. But at the same time it is important that the registration authority should have real and obvious independence, so that there is no suspicion of official influence at this critical point.

(b) *The onus of responsibility.* In designing a system a decision must first be taken about the onus of responsibility for registration. Is it to fall upon the voter or upon the administration? Is it assumed that the voter is a conscious and responsible citizen, and therefore that it is his business to decide whether or not to register? (Voters being what they are, this offers a premium to the well-organised party, which sees to it that its people get on the roll). Or is it assumed that it is the state's business to ensure that its elections are properly conducted, and therefore that the officials of the state should do all they can to see that all eligible voters are registered? This will of course be more expensive; and it may perhaps leave an opening for attacks by parties on the impartiality of officials.

On the whole, American tradition has leant to the first alternative, British to the second, at least since 1918. One result of American practice is that the number of voters registered is a good deal below the number of people who might be entitled to vote, and that participation in (for instance) an American Presidential election is a good deal lower than participation in a British general election. The records have it that in 1956 62 million Americans voted in the Presidential election out of an adult population of about 103 million (60%); in 1955 27 million British out of 35 million (77%) voted in a general election. The American figures are difficult to handle with precision, because electoral procedure is controlled by 48 different states; but the difference is certainly in part due to the failure of qualified persons to register, as well as to the failure of registered electors to vote.

Most American systems require the elector to take positive action at a date some time before the election. The rules are there, it is up to the elector to know them and obey them, and many electors fail to do so unless prompted by a party organisation. Much failure to register (for instance, by negroes in the South) is due to lack of an organisation prepared to encourage reluctant voters whose claim would in fact be upheld by the courts if they attempted to exercise it.

In the nineteenth century the British system also threw the onus on party organisers, but since 1918 there has been a legal obligation on the Registration Officer to conduct a house-to-house canvass. This is not construed quite literally. The actual procedure is that he arranges for a form of registration to be left at each house in his area, most electors return this form through the post (free of charge), a reminder is then sent to laggards, and door-to-door canvass is necessary only to deal with the small minority who still fail to reply. [1] How thorough this canvass is depends on the energy of the officials concerned, but British electoral registers are expensive (a register costs about £1,750,000) and are generally reckoned to be good. There is of course no outside standard by which to measure performance; but a registration of over 95% of eligible electors is certainly good, and the British standard is perhaps about 97% or 98%.

(c) *Periodical or permanent register*. This question of burden of responsibility takes rather different forms in two different systems of registration, quite distinct in theory, but overlapping in practice. One of these is the British system of periodical registers (these serve for local as well as for parliamentary elections). In principle, the British electoral register is scrapped each year and prepared afresh. The register in Great Britain is a record of those qualified to vote on 10th October in year A: it is effective for all elections on and after 16th February in year B; and remains effective until 15th February in year C. If this is construed literally it means that, in an extreme case, a person becoming qualified on 11th October in year A cannot claim to be registered until 10th October in year B, and cannot vote until 16th February in year C, about eighteen months after he became qualified. This may lead to rather dubious party manoeuvres, as the party in power has a measure of choice about the date of elections, both general elections and by-elections, and may choose to fight either on the 'old' register or on the 'new' register, according to its judgment of tactical advantage. Attempts have twice been made to improve the position by having two registers a year; but on both occasions the second register was dropped for reasons of economy, since it was of no use for local elections. There are, however, certain mitigations; a concession is made in favour of those reaching the

[1] The Manchester figures will serve as illustration: About 210,000 households, about 160,000 reply at first, another 30,000/35,000 after a reminder, leaving 12,000/15,000 to canvass.

age of 21 between 10th October in year A and 16th June in year B, who are placed on the register but cannot vote until an election occurring on or after 2nd October in year B, and arrangements for proxy and postal voting deal fairly well with the problem of voters moving from one constituency to another.

The principle of the continuous register is that the authorities keep a standing record of the body of electors, and are able to modify this at any time. In the perfect form of the system the record is a card-index of voters kept nationally and by constituencies. A voter's card is removed if he dies or emigrates: change of a woman voter's name is recorded when she marries: cards are moved from one constituency to another when there is a change of address: a new card is added for anyone reaching the age of 21 or otherwise becoming qualified. It will be obvious that this system goes well with an established system of national registration, an *état civil*. It would not be impossible to keep such a system for an electoral register alone, but it would be extravagant (except in dealing with a small electorate) unless the register could be made to serve more purposes than one. Hence the British (who adapt themselves well to queues but hate identity cards) are likely to adhere to the periodical register. The continuous register is equally well-established on the continent of Europe, where it is regarded as normal that everyone should have his 'papers', and it goes with a system of issuing to each voter a voter's card which is his 'document of identity' as a voter.

In spite of this sharp contrast in theory between the two systems the differences may be blurred in practice. In either system the onus of registration can be put either on the voter or on the state. The continuous registration system gives perhaps the best opportunity for action by the state, as elaborate arrangements can be made for those maintaining the register to be informed by other departments, as a matter of routine, about events affecting voters, such as death, sentences of imprisonment, certification as insane, or permanent emigration; and it should be possible in this way to keep a 'clean register' very efficiently. But the paper-work involved is enormous: and it is easier, even with a permanent register, to leave the initiative to individuals and parties.

The periodical register is perhaps less periodical than it seems, because officials generally work from the old register in compiling the new one, and find that over 80% of the names are unchanged from one year to the next,[1] a great saving in typing, checking and setting up type. Conversely, even the permanent register has seasonal peaks, because a central card-index, or even a constituency card-index, cannot be used for the management of an election on polling-day, and some arrangements must be made at some stage each year to print or duplicate

[1] In Manchester, an urban area with a relatively mobile population, about 62,000 a year drop off a register of 515,000, about 60,000 new names are added.

lists recording the position at a given date. This causes a much smaller time-lag, and leaves less room for party manoeuvres, than does the British system: but it does not avoid the difficulty completely.

Furthermore, it is convenient even with a periodical register to issue 'poll-cards' to the electors. These are not 'identity cards', their purpose is merely to help polling arrangements to go more smoothly, and they are not issued until an election is immediately in prospect. Yet they look not unlike the voters' cards issued under the other system.

As has been said above, the difference between the two systems is partly sentimental; some people do not like to think that they have been card-indexed. Sentiment apart, the choice is not easy, but it is essentially an administrative one, a problem of finding the system best suited to the type of electorate, the existing organisation of offices, the trend of work during the year, and the position about the recruitment of temporary staff for peak periods.

(d) *Provisional lists.* The nature of the electoral qualifications decides what burden of work and what sort of work fall on the Registration Officer and his staff at the stage of making up a provisional list.

If the system is one of universal franchise, or something near it, the job is mainly one of tiresome and difficult routine. Only a tiny proportion of claims to registration raises difficult issues, and disputed claims are relatively unimportant if the electorate is large. There are always some cases in which the Registration Officer has to take a *prima facie* decision for or against registration: but with a very large electorate his main difficulty is to organise his staff for checking, duplicating and printing so as to get accurate and legible work completed in the shortest possible time. It is simplest to cite the time-table for Great Britain as an example:

September or early October:	Forms sent out to all houses.
10th October:	Registration day.
Not later than 28th November:	Provisional printed registers available at Registration Offices and other centres.
16th December:	Closing date for appeals.
3rd January:	Completion of hearing of appeals.
As soon as possible after 3rd January:	Register published.
16th February:	Register in force.

It is an advantage of the British system that the work is done constituency by constituency, and in most areas there is an experienced nucleus of workers: on the other hand, a constituency may have as many as 75,000 voters, and the Registration Officer in a large town may be responsible for a number of constituencies. It is therefore unlikely that the work can be done much faster, at least with periodical registers.

The burden falls in rather a different place, if (as in nineteenth-century England or in some African countries) there is a 'qualitative' franchise with qualifications of an uncertain kind. In such circumstances the Registration Officer may have to deal with a larger number of difficult cases, and these may make up a larger proportion of the electorate. This is the main reason for choosing qualifications that prove themselves: to make the educational test 'possession of such-and-such a certificate' rather than 'capacity to understand English'; to make an income or property qualification 'possession of a receipt for tax of so much' or 'occupation of real property valued on the assessment roll at so much', rather than 'receipt of such-and-such an income' or 'ownership of real and movable property worth so much'. Choice of qualifications which leave a margin of doubt may have various bad effects. They may increase the burden on the senior administrative officials concerned so much that they have no time left for other work; they may perpetuate the state of paternalism which introduction of elections is designed to end, for voters may come to regard a vote as something which is in effect given them by the Registration Officer: in a rather more developed system of party warfare they leave the door open for corruption and for the suspicion of corruption (both equally serious), since so much depends on the 'length of the Registration Officer's foot'.

(e) *Appeals.* No system would be complete without some provision for appeal from the Registration Officer's decision to some independent authority, preferably a judicial authority. But the practicability of a system of appeals is controlled by two factors: the precision of the qualifications and the intensity of party warfare. Uncertain qualifications and hard fighting produce a high proportion of appeals; appeals must be dealt with speedily, or the whole work of registration is wasted, since a register becomes stale with delay; therefore, in such conditions, some special machinery for quick and cheap adjudication is required. In nineteenth-century England a case is quoted of 3,000 disputed cases on a register of 9,000 names; in a recent case in the Western Region of Nigeria there were some 12,000 disputed cases on a register which was eventually reduced to about 17,500 by 9,000 deletions (an exceptional example, in a constituency where tribal rivalry was strong). The British practice in the nineteenth century was to appoint temporary judges ad hoc, the 'Revising Barristers', chosen from the legal profession outside the constituency and remunerated by a fee for each day's sitting. Claims are now much less frequent, and revising barristers have not been appointed in Great Britain since 1918. Appeals now lie from the

Registration Officer to the County Court, and thence to the Court of Appeal, but not further.

In the nineteenth century the work of the Revising Barristers was onerous and not very satisfactory, because of the difficulty of obtaining consistent decisions from a number of judges not expert in this branch of law, acting independently of one another, under heavy pressure of work. Yet it is not easy to see how it could have been organised otherwise. Given a fairly small electorate, a loosely-defined franchise, and vigorous party warfare the pressure of disputes about registration is certain to be severe. It is at least better that it should be shared with some form of judicial body, rather than borne by the administration alone.

(f) *Late Registration.* Finally, there is the question whether any concessions can be made in favour of people qualified to vote whose names through no fault of their own do not appear on the final registers. This situation can arise with a permanent register from which electoral lists are compiled at intervals, as well as with the British system of periodical registers. The British make no concessions; no one can vote whose name is not on the register as printed and issued on the due date. The French are in this more elastic, and permit the last minute addition of names of officials and soldiers moved on transfer or demobilisation (up to ten days before poll), and of names omitted from the lists simply by a clerical error (up to the day of the poll). Applications must in each case be approved by a judge of first instance, the *juge de paix.* The procedure involved may be something of a nuisance to officials busy with other work for an impending election, but it is not difficult in itself, and doubtless the main reason for the lack of similar facilities in Britain is that there has been no vocal demand for them.

CHAPTER XIV

Polling Stations

1. *The Staff*

Each polling station must have a presiding officer, representative of the authority in charge of the election, and responsible to him both for the efficiency of his staff in following the routine prescribed and for the general conduct of business. It is rarely necessary to have much display of force on the spot; there may perhaps be one policeman in or near the station at the disposal of the presiding officer, but forces for dealing with serious trouble are best kept in reserve elsewhere.

What other staff is required is determined by the work to be done and the number of electors entitled to vote at that station. The most onerous part of the work is that of checking each voter against the register, establishing *prima facie* that he is the person who he claims to be, and issuing him with a ballot-paper or otherwise assisting him to vote. Voters do not arrive evenly throughout the day, there are many easy cases and a few difficult ones, and the pace at which clerks can work depends on their experience and competence. If we assume (purely as an example) that a good clerk working with the presiding officer can deal with 50 voters an hour, administrative conclusions follow about the level of staff needed in each polling station and also over the whole country. Thus an election with 30 million voters all voting on the same day within a polling period of 13 hours would need at least 46,000 'man-days' of clerical work, apart from presiding officers. This is a minimum, because some polling stations in sparsely populated areas will not work at full pressure, and because of the problem of peak periods. Voting is generally heavy in the morning and evening, at least in Western industrial countries, light in the middle of the day; some extra staff may be added for the evening, but at times voters must queue and wait.

The number of polling stations (and therefore of presiding officers) required is always a subject of some dispute, especially in rural constituencies. It is expensive both in cash and in manpower to increase the number of polling stations to such an extent that the staff of stations with small electorates sit idle for much of the day. On the other hand, it is not fair and equal that it should be more difficult for some voters than others to cast a vote. The percentage of votes cast is in general smaller in areas in which it is hard to get to a polling station, even though there are facilities for proxy voting or postal voting.

123

One method used in countries where population is scattered and communications poor is to spread voting over several days and to send 'polling teams' on circuit in rural areas, in order to open polling stations for short periods at a large number of different centres. This has a good many advantages, but creates some difficulties of its own, for instance about keeping unopened ballot-boxes after the poll in such a way that their security is above suspicion.

Whatever devices are adopted, an election requires an army of clerks which is quite large in relation to the voting population.[1] The simplest way to secure both staff and accommodation is that used in continental Europe—to hold elections on a Sunday. If this is impossible it will probably be necessary to close for the day a good many non-essential government offices, and it is also usual to close the schools (schools make useful polling stations) and to use many of the school-teachers as presiding officers and polling clerks. Many of the same staff can be used for counting the votes, which also requires a substantial army:[2] but it is a very hard day (though it is a useful way of earning a little extra money) for a clerk to go on from a twelve- or thirteen-hour day in a polling station to assist in the count.

It is usual to pay polling station and counting staff a fee for their day's work, even though they are already government employees, and this amounts to a large part of the cost of the election. The cost of the British election of 1955, with about 35 million people on the register, of whom 27 million voted, was about £1,000,000: of this much the largest part was fees to staff.

Where elections are well-established there are plenty of experienced people who know procedure well, and no special arrangements for training are needed, so long as the old procedure is followed. New recruits can pick it up by apprenticeship as they go. But some form of rehearsal is essential where the procedure is completely new: voting involves only a simple series of operations, but it is important to public confidence that the prescribed routine be followed carefully.

2. Lay-out and Equipment.

The lay-out of a polling station varies a little according to the voting procedure adopted, and this is dealt with in the next chapter. But the essentials are very simple: a table for each team of clerks, a few chairs, an adequately screened place where the voter can record his vote with confidence that he is not seen. This assurance of privacy is one essential: the other essentials are negative—that party emblems, party propaganda, spokesmen for one party or the other should be absolutely ex-

---

[1] The Manchester example will again serve to indicate scale: about 515,000 voters, 600 polling stations, 600 presiding officers, 1,200 clerks.
[2] Two clerks per 1,000 votes cast, in Manchester.

cluded from the polling station. Parties are often permitted to have one observer each within the polling station, to see fair play; there may be individual polling-agents for each party outside: but almost invariably meetings, demonstrations, and visual propaganda are banned within a certain distance. There is perhaps a certain symbolism in this contrast between (on the one hand) the noise and ostentation of the electoral campaign, on the other, the absolute bareness of the polling station, and the isolation of the voter within it.

3. *Procedure*

The voter entering a polling station is expected to claim that he is such-and-such a person and that his name is on the register. To make proceedings easier, he is often provided earlier with some sort of official card. In British procedure, the 'poll card' (formerly issued by the parties, now by the Registration Officer) is merely a ticket showing the name of the voter and his number on the register; if the voter has his poll card it is easy to find his name, if he has lost it he is not penalised except by waste of time and some grumbling. In other systems electors are issued with a card which is in a stricter sense a voting card, and they cannot vote unless they can produce it. Of course, if it has been lost they can obtain a duplicate: but this requires time and trouble, and it may not be possible to do it on election day.

Voters are generally assigned to a particular polling station and cannot vote at any other; the point of this is that each station should have its own section of the register, and should be responsible for checking the votes of voters on that section. It is possible to extend the voter's choice of station somewhat by giving alternatives, but only with increased risk of 'repeating' and of personation. It is difficult to check that a voter has not voted twice except by limiting him to a single station and marking the register there when he has voted. It has, however, become the practice in some countries where illiteracy is prevalent to mark the voter himself as well as the register, by requiring him to dip his thumb in gentian violet or some other stain which lasts for at least a day.

The voter cannot of course be expected to prove in the polling station that he is the person he claims to be. All that is required is a prompt and straightforward claim to be someone whose name is on the register, perhaps backed by the production of a poll card or voting card. It is not therefore difficult to impersonate another voter in an urban constituency where faces are not well known; the only effective check lies in the risk that the real voter has already voted. If a person arrives and claims a vote which has already been marked off on the register, and if he sticks to his story, the British practice is to permit him to vote, but on a ballot paper of a different colour. These doubtful votes (known as 'tendered votes') are set on one side; and if there are enough of them to be important (this rarely happens now) the result of the election will be settled at leisure by police enquiry and judicial decision. But 'tendered votes' must be investigated in any event: personation is a serious offence even if it does not affect the result.

CHAPTER XV

Voting and Counting the Votes

1. *Types of voting*

Voting may be open or secret; compulsory or optional; in person, by proxy or by post. The dominant form in all modern elections is personal voting by secret ballot, without compulsion, and this is dealt with in the second section of this chapter. The other variants are explained more briefly here.

(a) *Open voting* is now virtually obsolete in elections to legislative assemblies, even in societies where the level of literacy is low. The only important exceptions are found in indirect elections, in which it is not unusual for the lowest tier of elections, at village level, to be held in a very informal way. Indeed, it has sometimes proved difficult to induce villagers to trouble with the formality of a contested election at all, because (as they reasonably object) they have gone over the whole thing between themselves beforehand and know perfectly well whom they are going to choose. But open voting is of course normal in committees and small meetings of all sorts in Western societies, and it remains common in Trade Union practice, not so much in elections as in plebiscitary decisions for or against the acceptance of particular terms of employment. It is mainly in this last context that one now meets the traditional arguments for and against open voting.

The case against open voting is an obvious one. A voter cannot be held to account unless his vote is known; therefore, without open voting it is impossible to organise corruption or intimidation, either by a few powerful people or by the pressure of mass opinion. The case for it is of interest now largely because it was put forcibly by J. S. Mill, in his advocacy of *Representative Government*, and his arguments still have some relevance to the experience of compact social groups such as those formed by workers in industry.

Two arguments are used. First, it is absurd to suppose that the vote is a right, rather than a duty. A vote is a share in power to decide, it is therefore a form of power over others, and no man has a right to power, except in a narrow legal sense. 'Every such power, which he is allowed to possess, is morally, in the fullest force of the term, a trust'. A man's vote 'has no more to do with his personal wishes than the verdict of a juryman. It is strictly a matter of duty: he is bound to give it according

127

to his best and most conscientious opinion of the public good'[1]. If this is conceded, it is easy to see reasons why a man should do his duty openly in face of the public affected by it, since this is the most effective way of making him feel that he is accountable.

Secondly, secrecy of the ballot, however scrupulously observed, may give a wrong idea about the nature of political decisions. If there is at stake an issue of importance to a community, it is thrashed out, before the vote is taken, in discussion among people who have lived together for years. In any serious discussion of this kind the participants on one side and the other are familiar, their arguments, their interests, and their temperaments are known, and the waverers are also known. It does not help this process of opinion-making that discussion should be open, decision secret; no one knows then who has been convinced by what arguments, there may even be suspicion that people have said one thing in discussion, another by their vote. In fact, secret ballot may even hinder another kind of democratic process, that of reaching general agreement by open discussion—Quaker democracy, democracy which aims at decision by 'the sense of the meeting'.

These are real points, and it should certainly not be assumed that in all circumstances secret voting is better than open voting. But they are scarcely applicable to the characteristic situation of Western democracy, which is a democracy not of groups or communities, but of constituencies. The voters passing through a polling station do not in any effective sense constitute a social unit, they are not a 'public' to which a voter can reasonably be held responsible for his vote, and open voting would not contribute anything to the ethical value or social effectiveness of elections by constituencies. It is therefore natural that the other side of the argument should prevail. Open voting may lead to various abuses; if secrecy—and belief in secrecy—can be maintained, corruption is cut off at its source. Individual bribery and individual intimidation of electors are not now significant factors in Western elections: this is partly due to the great size of electorates, but the secrecy of the ballot is also important.

Forms of open voting need not therefore detain us long. The traditional practice, still the one followed spontaneously almost everywhere, is that of acclamation (or 'voice vote') followed by some other form of voting if the result remains in doubt. The presiding officer calls for 'those in favour?' 'those against?', there is a competition in clamour, and there is then a procedure for counting heads. This was the pattern of British parliamentary elections before the Ballot Act of 1872. The Returning Officer stood on the hustings with the candidates and their friends, the crowd assembled below, he presented each candidate in turn, and the candidate's friends in the mob shouted for him. Non-

[1] J. S. Mill: *Representative Government*, 1861 ed., pp. 191-2.

electors could shout as loud as electors, perhaps louder; indeed, procedure at the hustings was often an opportunity for the unenfranchised to make plain publicly which candidate they preferred. It was therefore necessary to appeal from voices to votes, and any candidate had the unqualified right to call for a poll. As observers of political conferences and other large gatherings know, the rules governing this right are often of critical importance in political management. If the platform has an unqualified right to decide as between competing shouts that 'the ayes have it', or 'the noes have it', this means that the bosses can control the decisions of the meeting. On the other hand, if everyone present can call for a poll or a division at any time proceedings may be obstructed interminably. This is a point of great importance in the development of procedure in assemblies of all kinds.

Assuming that procedure permits a simple appeal from acclamation, there are three possible ways of proceeding. One is for voters to file past the presiding officer individually and declare their choice, which he then marks in the 'poll-book': this was the traditional British system, open and accurate, but time-consuming. A second is for a show of hands or a show of cards or some other indication of choice: anyone who has attempted to make a count of even a small assembly voting in this way knows how confusing and unreliable such procedure is. Hence, the third method, that of division; the traditional method of the House of Commons, and also the method which seems to be invented quite spontaneously when elections are introduced at village level in small pre-literate societies. Division is of course impossible for a very large crowd; it is the ideal method for a small one, and (as was suggested in Chapter VII) (p. 54 n. 1) it can be used to produce the effects of quite subtle forms of voting such as the alternative vote and S.T.V.[1]

(b) *Compulsory voting.* It may be best to distinguish first between formal and informal, legal and extra-legal compulsion. In the absence of formal sanctions a registered elector is legally free to abstain from voting, but in deciding whether to vote or not to vote he is influenced by various motives and pressures. The turn-out depends on such factors as the amount of publicity given to the election, the effectiveness of canvassing by parties, the general attitude of the community. In tightly organised local communities it may sometimes be possible to speak of informal compulsion to vote, because the non-voter is an eccentric, a person who rejects the ordinary standards of the community, and who certainly suffers in various ways on account of his isolation. Various research studies confirm what is in any case to be expected, that there is

[1] Perhaps it should be added, for completeness, that some assemblies have 'push-button' voting: each member votes by pressing one of several buttons on his desk, his vote is recorded, and totals are flashed on a screen.

almost always, other things being equal, a higher turn-out of voters in small, compact, static communities than in large towns where many people are newcomers and constituency boundaries are no more than lines on a map.

The argument for compulsory voting is in effect that voting is a duty, and that the state should do what it can to reinforce the social pressure (or moral obligation) to vote. The word 'apathy' is perhaps misleading: an elector can be apathetic in voting as well as in not voting—indeed, it is possible to abstain from voting in a purposeful way. The rationale of compulsory voting is that it is in all circumstances better to vote (even apathetically) than not to vote. The earliest example of this reasoning is to be found in a law said to have been enacted by Solon, at Athens in the sixth century B.C., which required that if there were civil strife in the state all citizens must join one side or the other, under penalty of disfranchisement, since the abstention of a large mass of citizens[1] favoured tyranny.

This is certainly as true now as in Athens 2,500 years ago: but it has never been shown that enactment of penalties is an effective remedy.

If compulsory voting is to be introduced, it is not difficult to arrange. There is in any event a record at the polling station of those who have voted: a penalty is imposed automatically on all non-voters who cannot produce a valid excuse, such as ill-health or absence on important business. The penalty cannot be large, since substantial numbers of people are involved; it might of course be stepped up to penalise persistent offenders, but this would give an embarrassing opportunity to martyrs—it has not been tried in Australia, the scene of the only notable experiment in compulsory voting.

The case against compulsory voting is therefore one of principle rather than of practice. There are two points. First, there is the old argument, that law cannot safely run far ahead of the ordinary man's feelings about what is right. If opinion is not such as to enforce voting informally, it will not tolerate its enforcement formally by penalties high enough to be effective; and ineffective or unenforceable penalties weaken respect for law. As usual, this argument proves too much, as it proves that formal sanctions are always either unnecessary or ineffective: in this matter, as in others, it is probable that a penalty judiciously chosen and enforced can move waverers in the direction derived.

It is perhaps more important (secondly) that there is generally felt to be a certain incompatibility of principle between compulsory voting and free elections. This is not perfectly logical—there can be free choice about how to cast a compulsory vote—but it is extremely persua-

[1] 'Good easy people who like to have things decided for them': Aristotle: *Constitution of Athens*, VII. 5.

sive. It seems to most people reasonable that one of the democratic liberties is to decline to vote for any of the alternatives offered: it is in fact assumed that the vote is a right, not a duty, and fluctuations in turnout are always held to be as important an indication of opinion as fluctuations in the votes for parties. Even if there is compulsory voting, this general dissent may express itself through the propertion of 'spoiled papers' handed in. It is hard to penalise the spoiling of voting papers, as deliberate choice can rarely be proved: therefore, why trouble to attempt to restrain a kind of freedom which will assert itself in any case?

None of these arguments apply to the special case of informal compulsion by organs of the state in 'elections by acclamation', a type of 'unfree' election referred to in the final chapter of this book.

(c) *Proxy voting* is not a matter which has ever been of first-rate importance except in the House of Lords and in the management of limited liability companies. Presumably it was not used in the earliest English elections because of the tradition that an election was a public meeting: similarly it was not used in elections to the French States General except for women property-owners qualified to vote in their own right, who could act politically only through a male proxy. In modern elections its scope is limited to the case of voters necessarily absent from the poll in circumstances such that it is difficult for them to vote by post. This was important in Britain at the elections of 1918 and 1945, which took place when many voters were still on service at distant stations overseas. Present British electoral law limits the use of proxies to members of the armed forces and to civilians likely to be at sea or abroad on the day of the poll because of their jobs or as members of auxiliary forces. Similar principles govern proxy voting eleswhere.

The administrative problems of proxy voting are: first, the authentication by the voter of a form of proxy, secondly, the acceptance of the form as valid by the Registration Officer, thirdly, setting an appropriate mark opposite the voter's name in the register—and this means that registration of proxies (though it need not be done when the register is made up) must be complete a little time before the election (in Britain not later than nomination day, nine working days before the poll). Finally, there must be a check to see that there has not been a muddle leading to double voting: it would be unfortunate that registration of a proxy should prevent an elector voting in person if he managed unexpectedly to arrive in time for polling-day, and this right can only be given if there is a proper check to ensure that his vote is not cast twice.

All this is perhaps of symbolic rather than practical importance. Proxy votes can seldom affect the result of a modern election: but elaborate arrangements are made for them lest any elector feel that he has been excluded through no fault of his own.

(d) *Postal voting* may be much more important, and it is not easy to decide how freely it should be allowed. The case for it is that the opportunity to vote should be given as generously as possible; the case against it is that postal voting on the whole favours the most literate voters and the best organised party machines.

First, one can set on one side constituencies where voting is solely (or mainly) by post: the only important cases are those of the British University constituencies from 1918 to 1950, and the (still existing) 'graduates' constituency in the Sudan. [1] These raise no special questions of procedure not referred to below.

Next, there is the question who, in an ordinary constituency, should be entitled to vote by post. The strongest cases are those of people who are temporarily absent from the constituency at the time of the election, who have moved permanently from the constituency since the register was compiled, or who are present in the constituency but find it difficult or impossible to reach a polling station, because of ill-health or because of lack of means of transport. Postal voting was introduced in Britain on a small scale in 1918; in 1945 it was extended to most of the cases mentioned. But absence from the constituency is not reckoned a good reason unless it is regular absence on public or private business (not pleasure), and able-bodied people in the constituency are expected to be able to reach polling-stations except in a few cases of islands and indented coasts, where outlying voters are cut off from the polling stations by the sea. It is unlikely that these rules will be relaxed much further in a country like Britain. It might be argued that in sparsely populated countries anyone who wishes should be entitled to vote by post, but the administrative difficulties would be considerable.

The administrative problems may be set out briefly as follows:—

(i) It is essential that postal voters should be marked on the register, in order to ensure that the vote is not used twice, and also so that the necessary voting forms can be sent to them in time. This means that the right to a postal vote must be claimed a reasonable time before election day: nine working days, in British practice. If this period is kept relatively short it means that adjudication on entitlement must be in the hands of the Registration Officer. Provisions for appeal could hardly be made effective in time for the election.

(ii) It is virtually essential that postal voting should be carried out carefully on forms officially provided. A loose procedure would leave room for abuses and suspicion; on the other hand a strict procedure

---

[1] There is also a University constituency with postal voting which returns four members by S.T.V. to the House of Commons of Northern Ireland, which has 52 members. In the Republic of Ireland there are six University members in the Senate, elected by postal voting.

means that a good deal of office work is involved, and also that the voter must either be reasonably good at dealing with forms or must get advice from some one who is.

(iii) Difficulties arise about the combination of authentication with secrecy. This is, however, possible with some of the forms of voting referred to in the next section, those in which the voter chooses either by marking a ballot paper or by choosing (and perhaps also marking) one of a number of lists. A postal voter in these cases receives by post the necessary papers with an envelope and a form of authentication. He places his vote in the envelope, seals it, and then completes the authentication form in the presence of a witness who also signs. The voting envelope and the authentication are then both enclosed in a larger envelope, which goes by post to the Returning Officer. A clerk opens the outer envelope, checks the correctness of the authentication, and then puts the voting envelope unopened in a box to be dealt with separately. The ballot-papers (which are not identifiable except in so far as any ballot-paper is identifiable) are thus separated completely from the authentication forms which bear the voters' names, and there is no real danger to secrecy, so long as the clerical processes are properly supervised. It may, however, happen that postal votes are not effectively mixed with other votes before counting, so that party managers have a good general idea, officially or unofficially, how the postal vote has gone. Information thus obtained confirms the expectation that those who take the trouble to vote by post are not a random sample of the electorate, and that postal voting thus favours some parties more than others. It has been claimed, quite plausibly, that better use of the postal vote by the Conservatives in the British general election of 1951 enabled them to gain ten marginal seats, and that this decided an election which gave them a majority of seventeen over all other parties in the House of Commons.

2. *Personal voting by secret ballot*

The mechanics of voting are affected to some extent by the choice between the systems sketched in Part Two of this book; for instance, S.T.V. is generally associated with a standard official ballot-paper with spaces in which the voter puts the figures 1, 2, 3 and so on. But even that is not an absolute rule—in minor elections S.T.V. can be operated by permitting voters to write down the candidates' names in their order of preference—and it is quite fair to separate problems about the mechanics of voting from problems about systems of voting.

There are four main types of procedure: one on which the voter chooses between ballot-boxes; one in which he marks an official paper, identical in form for all voters, and drops it in a single box; one in which he chooses the paper he prefers out of several (official or unofficial) and drops the chosen paper in a single box; and voting by machine. These methods can of course be combined in various ways.

(a) *Choice of boxes*. In a sense, this is the oldest and strictest form of 'balloting'. Ballots in the literal sense are small balls, used either for drawing lots or for voting. 'Ballots' used for voting were all identical, and a voter chose by dropping his ballot into the appropriate urn. The form of voting was 'secret ballot' if the voter's choice was kept secret, either by screening the boxes, or by constructing a box which the voter could slip his hand and choose one of several compartments inside, or by a system of 'black balls' and 'white balls', by which the voter could slip one ball into the voting urn, the other into an urn for discarded ballots. This system emerged in various forms in many places, in the ancient Republic of Athens, in the Renaissance Republic of Venice, in the proceedings of the Catholic Church; and it is curious that the political scientist James Harrington found in it a remedy for most of England's troubles in the 1650s, just as J. S. Mill took refuge in S.T.V. in the 1850s.

This ancient method has become popular again in recent years because it is the best way of giving secrecy to the vote in countries where the literacy rate is low. Since 1945 choice of boxes has virtually become standard practice in Africa, India and South East Asia. The voter, once identified by the register, is given an official ballot-paper. Careful security precautions must be taken to see that the ballot-papers contain some feature not known and not readily copied by an outside printer: and there is an effective extra check against spurious papers if each paper is stamped with some private mark by the clerk as he hands it to the voter. The voter then retires alone behind a screen into a compartment in which he finds several boxes, each marked with the name of a party, the name (and perhaps the photograph) of its candidate (or candidates), and an easily remembered symbol—cock, lion, palm-tree, spinning-wheel, spade, and so on. It is important that there should be good lighting in the place of voting, that boxes should not be blocked by ill-folded papers, or by other objects put in by malicious persons, and that the boxes should not be placed so that the voter comes more easily to one than to the others. The voter drops his paper into the box which he chooses: or at least he ought to do so—he may be under some temptation to secrete it and sell it for a small sum to a party organiser outside, who will later get someone to cast several ballots at once. This can be discouraged by watching voters carefully as they enter and leave, but it cannot be stopped entirely without infringing the privacy of the voting compartment. Such small scale cheating cannot affect the results much in large electorates, but it may have a bad effect on standards of public morality.

This system has given rise to a good many rules about the allocation of symbols to parties. Party propaganda is out of place within the polling station, but what about the persuasive effects of symbols ? It is a general rule that no party should be allowed to choose a symbol which is revered throughout the community—the cow in India, for instance—and which might therefore enable it to marshal sentiment of an irrelevant kind. Some countries go so far as to produce official symbols and to allocate them by lot between parties. But it is clearly not practicable to do this afresh for each election, since the working of the system depends on the creation by mass propaganda of a close association in the minds of voters between symbol, party name, party attitude or policy, and party candidate, and if such propaganda is to be effective, it must be continuous. The political use of a visual image in this way may seem odd to those who live in literate societies, but it is familiar to them in all forms of commercial advertising, and in principle there is no line to be drawn between association with an image (such as 'lion') and association with a word (such as 'labour') or a colour (such as red).

This may be a convenient point at which to mention a transitional form of semi-secret voting, the 'whispered vote'. Secret voting by symbol is really practicable only where the administration is capable of methodical organisation on quite a large scale and there are parties which have reached the stage of mass campaigning. The only effective way of protecting the privacy of the voter in societies which have not reached this stage is an extremely 'paternal' or 'colonial' one. The District Commissioner (or his representative—preferably white) sits apart at a table, the voters approach him one by one and tell him in a low voice how they wish to vote, he marks the vote (without a name) on a sheet out of sight of the audience. There is nothing wrong with this system except that it postulates a rather unusual and temporary combination of circumstances; circumstances in which it is desired to go forward from traditional forms of government to voting, yet there is still a paternal 'white man' accepted as being impartial, above and outside the system, a good custodian of secrets because he does not really understand them.

(b) *Marking a voting-paper.* The second main method is that by which an official voting-paper is given to each elector; he signifies his choice by marking the paper, and then drops it in the box, or folds it or places it in an envelope and gives it to an official to drop in the box. The paper maybe a very simple one, as in the plurality system, in which the voter need only place X opposite the candidate of his choice; rather more elaborate choice may be possible, as under S.T.V.; or the paper may include several lists of parties and candidates, and the voter is entitled to perform various different operations, if the system is one of list voting with preferential voting and *panachage*. It is also possible to conduct several elections on one piece of paper, by asking a voter (for instance) to choose a member for a federal parliament and a member of a regional or state parliament, and also to vote for or against some specific proposal submitted in a referendum. There is no limit to possible variations except common sense: to submit too many questions at once may produce not effective choice but either confusion or a premium in favour of the best drilled party.

In a system dependent on markings officials are bound to discourage the use of anything except an official voting-paper, because of the trouble that may arise in counting. Indeed, there is always a certain amount of difficulty over 'spoiled papers'; naturally, the proportion increases with the complexity of the system, and if it is relatively high it may cause serious trouble in the process of counting votes. Administrative difficulties arise not over papers that are clearly 'spoiled' but over marginal cases, since someone must give a judgment on each of them, with reasonable care and uniformity, under the critical eye of observers interested in party advantage.

The British practice is that official voting-papers are numbered, and the number of the paper issued is marked opposite the voter's name in the register. This is in principle a breach of secrecy of the ballot: in practice, complete security is maintained, because the marked register is sealed separately from the ballot-boxes when the poll closes, the register, ballot-papers and counterfoils are sent under seal to a judicial official, the Clerk of the Crown in Chancery, are destroyed at the end of one year, and during that year may be consulted only on the order of the High Court in the course of a judicial enquiry. It is not essential that ballot-papers be numbered, but unless this is done fraud cannot be effectively pursued in a system of secret ballot. The decision therefore involves a certain amount of judgment about the greater risk—the risk of loss of confidence and secrecy, or the risk of undetected fraud.

The system of the 'official mark' arose out of a type of fraud invented shortly after the passage of the Ballot Act. An agent managing corrupt voters would send his first man in to hand to the official a dummy ballot-paper in place of the real paper, which he brought out to his paymaster. This would be marked and given to the second man, who would see that it was placed in the box and would bring out his own paper unmarked, as evidence against which he could claim his reward in cash. The process could continue all day through a chain of voters, and might be of some importance so long as electorates were fairly small. The official counter-move was to stamp ballot-papers immediately before issue with a secret imprint, settled only that day, which could be seen even when the paper was folded. The folded paper was to be shown to the clerk for identification of the imprint before it was put in the box: and this made impossible (except by good fortune or extreme ingenuity) the first step in the chain, the first corrupt voter bearing a dummy paper.

Another problem, which recurs in different systems of voting, is that there are always some voters who do the easiest thing. In a system of marking ballot-papers, there is always a slight bias in favour of the first name on the paper; similarly, there will be a slight bias in favour of the box most easily found, of the lever most easily accessible on a voting-machine. The bias is trivial if the voter has a straightforward choice, for instance, between two men or two parties: it may be of some importance if there is a long and confusing list of names from which to choose—a 'drift' of even 1 per cent or 2 per cent of voters to the first name on the list may then be decisive.

The rule most commonly followed is to make up the list in alphabetical order of candidates or of parties. But if the bias becomes important parties in choosing candidates begin to show a preference for the early letters of the alphabet, and the randomness of the order is upset. Hence it may be decided to settle the order by drawing names at random: or to print sets of papers each giving the names in a different order, and to issue papers to successive voters from each set in turn.

(c) *Choice of voting-papers*. The next system is one in which alternative choices are printed separately on different pieces of paper: the voter chooses the piece of paper which he favours and drops it in the box. This may be used in single-member constituencies, but is more often associated with list systems of P.R., in which the voter chooses the list he prefers, and with the old American 'long ballot' system, in which the voter votes simultaneously in a series of simple plurality elections for a variety of offices (and perhaps in referenda as well), and expects to be supplied by the party of his choice with a 'slate' or 'ticket' covering the whole range of voting. Both systems may also admit marking by the voter: the voter may in some way add to, alter, or delete from the piece of paper offered by the party.

Under this system the papers are generally printed by the parties, subject to official regulations about their form and contents. In some countries the voter finds various party agents outside the polling station or elsewhere, who seek to thrust their lists into his hand: he can of course preserve his privacy by accepting copies of them all, and making his choice inside, but the situation is a somewhat embarrassing one, and can be avoided by setting out piles of ballots in the polling station from which the voter can make his choice more privately. There is also the risk that a voter may attempt to stuff more than one list into the ballot-box: this can be met fairly effectively by the arrangement that all lists are to be the same in form, the voter is to put his chosen list in an official envelope, and that if at the count more lists than one are found in a single envelope they are all invalid.

(d) *Machine voting* has become almost universal in the U.S.A. It is particularly suitable to American practice, under which (even with a relatively short ballot) the voter votes in several elections at once under a plurality system. A typical machine is laid out in columns: at the top of each column is a plain statement of the office or decision which it represents: below it in each column are buttons or levers, each representing a possible choice in that election. The voter enters the curtained booth, pulls or pushes a main lever which makes the machine 'live', moves the lever of his choice in each column (leaving some alone if he prefers to do so), moves the main lever again to lock the machine and register his votes, then withdraws. The machine is no more than an adding machine, certified and sealed before proceedings begin; it records the votes as they are made, and all that is required in 'counting' is to unseal the machine with due precautions and look at the dials.

Europeans perhaps regard this mechanisation as typically American and a trifle absurd. There is, however, a great deal to be said for it, on the scores of saving of labour, gain in accuracy, avoidance of spoiled votes, and secrecy. Most American machines are designed for particular systems of voting in which the voter's choice is limited. It is, however, a relatively simple business to design machines which will deal with any of the forms of voting described in Part Two; so long as the voter is not allowed to *add* names to those indicated for him, he can play tunes on a machine almost as various as those that can be played on a piano, and the machine (if it has not been tampered with) will combine his choice with that of other voters to produce a verdict with perfect speed and accuracy. But machines, even relatively simple ones, are expensive; polling clerks cannot be dispensed with, because the voter must be identified, and probably the expense of voting by machine is as great as the cost of printing and counting ballot-papers, except in a country where labour costs are very high and elections are very frequent.

3. *Miscellaneous questions of security*

There are a number of minor points, of some importance in themselves, which can perhaps best be introduced at this point.

(a) *Security of the ballot-boxes.* One of the best-established ways of cheating in an election is to 'stuff' the ballot-boxes, by inserting at some stage large numbers of papers not submitted by genuine electors. It is generally possible for all parties to keep an eye on the ballot-boxes during the period of polling: the weak points are before and after that period. To ensure that ballot-boxes are not 'stuffed' beforehand, the usual practice is that there should be a small piece of formality at each polling station when it opens for the day. The presiding officer shows the ballot-boxes, open and empty, to the representatives of the candidates and to any members of the public who are present: he then seals them formally in such a way that papers can be inserted only through the proper openings in the lids. There is a similar formality at the end of the poll, if the votes are not counted at once: the openings in the ballot-boxes are then closed and officially sealed, and it is the presiding officer's responsibility to see that the sealed boxes are delivered intact to the Returning Officer at the place appointed. This may be a serious matter where corruption is endemic, and it is physically onerous in large constituencies with poor communications; in some African constituencies the presiding officer and a few policemen have to carry the boxes on foot through difficult country for thirty or forty miles.

(b) *Persuasion within the polling station.* We have already remarked that it is taken as a point of principle that the voter, though open to propaganda during the campaign, must be left to make his final choice in peace. The polling station and procedure there belong to the state, which is neutral between the contending parties. The simple voter may cast round anxiously for an indication how the powers that be wish him to vote, and it is important that he should not be given it. The emblems of the state displayed in the polling station must not be such that they seem to favour one party in particular: no party must be given special favours as regards what it may display. The usual rule is that no party material of any kind is admitted into the polling station or within a specified distance of it: even more important, persons representing the parties are excluded from this area, with the exception (in some systems) of one polling-agent to represent each candidate, who is allowed to be present (subject to strict rules of behaviour) and to satisfy himself that business is being done properly.

There remains the question of the official voting-papers themselves, if these are used. How much should they show? Simply the names of the candidates? Their names and the names of their parties? Some brief description or biography by which the voter may recognise them? The matter becomes even more complex in referenda on bills or constitutional amendments, when the bare title may be meaningless to the average elector, and the full legal draft is just as bad. Is space to be given for a summary? But are not all summaries tendencious? These are unanswerable questions, which can be dealt with well enough in a common-sense way. Perhaps the British lack common sense, in that their ballot-papers show the names and occupations of candidates, but not the names of parties, and it is common enough for a simple elector to emerge baffled from the booth to ask the presiding officer which candidate is which: the official is not allowed to tell him, but must send him outside to enquire from a party henchman at the door. One result of this official affectation of indifference to parties is that a local electoral campaign must spend much effort simply on teaching faithful party voters, by constant repetition, what the name of their candidate is, lest good votes be thrown away. It would clearly be wise and safe in a British election to print party labels on the papers, and this would not constitute a precedent for more extreme steps.

(c) *Assistance to voters.* There are always a few voters physically fit to get to the polling stations and mentally capable of understanding the issues but not able to record their votes without assistance. The most obvious category is that of blind persons; there may also be some cripples, and there are illiterates voting under a system (such as that of marking voting-papers) which makes no concessions to illiteracy. This is a matter (like proxy voting) which is of importance in principle rather than in substance, and there are two obvious ways of dealing with it. One is to permit the helpless person to be assisted by a 'friend', who may be permitted to enter the screened compartment with the voter and if necessary to make his mark for him; the other is for the presiding officer to act in the same way.

4. *Counting the votes*

The mechanics of counting depend largely on the system of voting adopted, and there are only a few general points to be made here.

Under some systems the counting is done in each station at the close of the poll. The boxes are opened, the presiding officer and his assistants compile their returns in the presence of party representatives who are there to see fair play, the figures are entered up on the official forms, and the forms are sent to the central point of decision, along with 'spoiled papers' or any other 'exhibits' which may be important in a dispute. This is the most natural method with machine voting; its disadvantages are that it may involve some breach of secrecy in small communities (there will be a good deal of speculation if the votes for each party do not come out as expected in a hamlet with (say) 25 votes), and that arrangements for supervision depend on the efficiency of local party observers, and are of necessity rather haphazard. Local counting need not involve delay, since the results of local counting can be transmitted at once to the central point at which the results are decided. In P.R. with a national pool many of the results must in any event be computed at the centre, from figures submitted by local counting stations.

The security of the count, if it is centralised, depends partly on the fact that it is a routine clerical operation carried out at top speed by trained clerks, and that the nature of the routine and the checks built into it should be such as to make errors or deliberate falsification virtually impossible except by collusion between a large number of people: partly on the presence of candidates and their agents during the count, so that there is effective publicity. The operation requires some skill in office organisation, and it may go wrong in inexperienced hands; or an unscrupulous Returning Officer might create a muddle and use it to improve the chances of one candidate against another's. But the actual counting is in some ways the easiest part of elections to keep honest.

The greatest difficulty is that of finding a uniform and reliable procedure for sorting out ballot papers which are in some way abnormal, and may give indications of dishonesty or may be invalid for reasons of form. There are two stages in the problem. The first is the action of the routine counting clerk: what line does he take in putting on one side doubtful or ambiguous papers? The second is that of the officer in charge, to whom doubtful papers are referred for a decision. Those concerned are in a position to twist procedure one way or the other, and if anyone plans dishonesty at the polling stations, he is also interested in the control of the count. To 'steal' an election successfully it is necessary to exercise influence at both levels.

There are a number of other matters which are important only if the election is very closely contested, but may then raise curious technical difficulties. If the margin is narrow it is usual to have a re-count: but who is entitled to call for a recount, in what circumstances, and how many times may the count be repeated? It is also important in such a case to have an opportunity for appeal to a court about spoilt papers which are in dispute: but how is this to be done fairly and expeditiously? There may even be difficulties in interpreting the electoral law not foreseen by those who drafted it. Where the alternative vote or second ballot is used the statute may require in certain circumstances an 'absolute majority', and the phrase may never require closer definition until a case arises in which the result depends on a margin of five or ten votes. It is then important to know whether 'absolute majority' means a majority of votes submitted or of votes *validly* submitted (excluding spoilt papers). It is never possible to clear up all such difficulties by regulation in advance: like any other machine, a newly-designed electoral system develops 'bugs' (as engineers say) which are gradually eliminated by experience.

Part Four: Electoral Morality and its Enforcement

CHAPTER XVI

The Main Issues

The first two parts of this book dealt with the structure of electoral systems, the third with common elements in the administration of elections. A specified electoral system has no political existence unless it is administered in a way which corresponds pretty closely to its specification. Exact correspondence is impossible, since life and law never are and never can be identical: a little divergence from legal form gives life to a system, much divergence transforms it, very great divergence modifies it so radically that it is destroyed, and nothing remains of it but empty words.

Thus the administrative problems described are one of the factors which control the nature of a system. It can work as theory requires only if there is an administrative organisation to make it work. Part Three constitutes a very elementary treatise on how to run elections; by implication it is also an elementary treatise on how to cheat in elections, because the key points in administration are the key points of attack for ill-disposed persons anxious to falsify the returns and distort the system.

Cheating of this sort depends on direct falsification. If the administration is corrupt, feeble and incompetent, such falsification is easy, and, because it is easy, it readily becomes endemic. But it is also relatively easy to control, because it is easy to define and identify, and because checks of a simple kind can be built into the administrative structure. If administration is bad, there is a descending spiral: parties all cheat alike and elections quickly deteriorate into farce. But if administration is even moderately good, the spiral runs the other way; the parties become auxiliaries of public order, since they watch one another, and the chance of cheating undetected is very small. This is the stage reached in most Western countries; electoral administration is very careful and precise, and controversy about this sort of electoral corruption is almost extinct.

But, important as this is, it is a relatively small part of the story. Three factors are involved. In Part Two we are concerned with arguments about fairness or unfairness in the specification of the electoral system; in Part Three with fairness or unfairness in the way it is administered. A fairly administered system might be most unfair in its specification (some people say this of the British system). But even if it

is admitted that the system is fair and its administration is fair, it may
still be alleged that elections held under it are not free, because conditions exist which limit the freedom of some of the parties. To discuss
this third factor one must go beyond the mechanics of the way in which
votes once cast are translated into seats gained; one must discuss the
freedom of the voter to cast his vote as he wishes.

To pursue this discussion far leads into deep waters:

> 'Fixt fate, free will, foreknowledge absolute . . .
> 'A gulf profound as that *Serbonian* bog
> Betwixt *Damiata* and mount *Casius* old,
> Where Armies whole have sunk.'

But one or two simple points may perhaps serve as common ground
for practical discussion.

First, it is obvious that 'free' elections cannot take place in an 'unfree'
society. If we set to work to define 'free' and 'unfree' precisely, we are
bound to find that in practice these are relative terms: no country can
ever in practice conform so exactly to a definition as to be either wholly
'free' or wholly 'unfree' (unless the definition treats the word 'free' as
no more than an ornamental epithet which certain individuals or peoples
inherit by birth—since 'Britons never never shall be slaves'). But there
is a plain sense, familiar since the eighteenth century, in which political
liberties depend on civil liberties. Elections cannot be (even relatively)
free unless civil liberties are (at least relatively) secure.

What is meant by civil liberties can be described either in terms of
social climate or in terms of legal rights and safeguards. The climate
of liberty is one in which a great deal of miscellaneous information
about public affairs circulates widely, what is heard or read is discussed
generally, and men join together in informal or formal organisations to
further their opinions about it. The law of civil liberty includes such
topics as freedom of speech, freedom of the press, freedom of public
meeting, freedom of peaceful organisation, freedom from the imposition
of penalties such as imprisonment or financial loss except by the
sentence of a court acting on known law.

It is agreed that all these freedoms must in some sense be limited,
in order to prevent individuals from damaging one another maliciously
and to secure the orderly conduct of business: it is also agreed that
limitations imposed for these reasons must not be used to obtain political
advantages for those who constitute the government for the time being.
This balanced argument about the defence and limitation of freedom
can become very complex: its complexities can be used maliciously to
spread confusion and distrust; but perhaps, for those who enter the
argument honestly and seriously, it is common ground that the right to
govern rests in consent, and that consent can only be given by people

who understand (or at least have equal opportunities to understand) what choice is offered to them.

If these very wide propositions are accepted, the next stage in the argument is to apply them to the regulation of electoral morality.

An election is not free unless voters vote freely. How is this to be defined? No one now believes that rational freedom (in an eighteenth-century sense) ever has been or ever can be completely achieved in practice. It remains an ideal that the enlightened citizen should decide rationally at the polls, after weighing all available information, on a choice between persons or issues clearly presented to him. But we know that in all electoral systems most voters vote as members of their party, of their social group or class, of their tribe, of their local community, that their intellectual horizon is limited and that their social situation influences their votes. Social bonds contend with rational choice. But if we acknowledge the strength of social bonds we do not thereby deny the right of the individual to break them. The strength and continuity of society depend in part on what Bagehot called 'the cake of custom': but they depend also on intelligent adaptation to changing circumstances, and this can come about only through intelligent choice by individuals, since only individuals possess intelligence.

It follows that in political action the voter should be free from certain forms of explicit compulsion. The most obvious freedoms are that his vote should not be influenced by intimidation or by bribery: that is to say, he should not be penalised or rewarded for his vote as an individual, apart from his share in its public consequences.

Organised force and the power of great wealth should not be employed to influence individual voters, because this destroys the nature of the vote. But is it not equally improper that intimidation and bribery should influence the voters as a whole? This is a more difficult problem. Organised force and money which can be spent freely constitute the springs of power in a society: no social act—and voting is a social act—can be completely insulated from their influence. Yet it is a fundamental proposition in this system of thought that elections are not free if those in power can manipulate them so as to perpetuate their own power; free elections are essentially a device for the legitimation and limitation of power. Hence there arise more difficult questions, which cannot be avoided: what limits are to be set to the use of mass organisation to impress the electors with a sense of their individual helplessness, to the use of wealth to control sources of information and so to conceal or distort the choice offered?

Hitherto we have been dealing with questions well-worn by experience, in Part Four the issues are more open, and it would not be right to claim that there is anywhere a system which satisfies all the criteria of freedom. But in some countries the questions here sketched are known to be real and urgent, and the attempt to answer them is a point of growth in the politics of democracy.

It is convenient for exposition to set matters out as follows: Chapter XVII deals with questions of organised force: intimidation of the individual elector, and the use of mass organisation to influence the electorate as a whole. Chapter XVIII deals with corruption, the use of money and other inducements to bribe individuals, Chapter XIX with the influence of wealth in a wider sense.

CHAPTER XVII

Intimidation and Public Order

1. *Pressure on individuals*

An individual may be influenced in his vote by threats of personal violence to himself or those to whom he is attached, or by threats of economic and social sanctions such as boycotting. Private violence, or the threat of it, is a crime under any system of law worthy of the name, and requires no special electoral legislation. Other sanctions are usually not forbidden in general terms; indeed the boycott and the strike are held to be weapons of the under-dog rather than of the powers that control physical resources of wealth and weapons, and complete prohibition of organisations using such sanctions is one of the marks of dictatorship. In spite of this difficulty, it is easy enough to legislate that the use of any threat designed to influence the vote of an individual is improper: and most electoral codes include such a provision.

The difficulty is to enforce it. How can one frame a law in terms precise enough to justify action by the police and the courts? For instance, it was well understood in eighteenth- and nineteenth-century England that the tenant of a farm should vote in his landlord's 'interest'; some landlords were tolerant, but most expected and secured obedience. Was this due to 'improper' pressure? Most tenancies were from year to year, and could be terminated quite legally on short notice: how was the law to distinguish the landlord's use of discretion in managing his own property from his use of property to influence votes? Explicit sanctions of this sort merge imperceptibly into a general system of social sanctions and social conformity. Certain pressures make it inconvenient for permanent civil servants in Britain to be avowed members of the Communist Party, which is not an illegal organisation; other pressures make it difficult for a working coal miner to be an avowed Conservative. Such social pressure is rarely directed so specifically to the question of voting that electoral law can be brought into play.

There are, however, three things which may help a little to redress the balance. One is provision for the secret ballot: its power is real, even though it only defends the individual who is prepared to defend himself by dissimulation. A second requirement is that there should be independent courts freely open to individuals strong-minded enough to use them, and that the courts should take a strict view in any case when there is an allegation of improper pressure. In the third place, if parties exist which compete on a national scale, each of them gives countenance and support to possible sympathisers isolated in a milieu unfavourable to them. A combination of these three factors gives reasonable scope to the dissenter: but they cannot in themselves protect him completely. It is idle to think that there can be the same degree of independence in a society of village communities as there is in a great metropolis. Electoral law cannot create a higher degree of individual responsibility than the nature of society permits: the most it can do is to strengthen a trend towards individual decision in face of forces which tell against it.

2. *Mass Intimidation*

In a sense, any large organisation is alarming. The scale of modern political parties dwarfs the individual, and the mere existence of great parties discourages the efforts of smaller ones. But large parties (or parties ambitious to become large) have open to them a choice of tactics. They may seek to be persuasive, or they may seek to be imposing.

The rules of action for a party which seeks to impose itself are now familiar. Those which would generally be accepted as legitimate are the summoning of large meetings in public open spaces, processions through the streets with banners, a large expenditure on posters, the wearing of badges and the display of window cards by supporters. These things make possible a display of strength, sometimes on a very large scale, but they do not threaten formally the state's monopoly of force. Threats to create a state within a state were the mark of Fascism and Nazism during their rise in the 1920s, and in most countries such action is now illegal. Examples of it are the adoption of party uniforms which travesty military or police uniforms: the creation of para-military organisations within the party; public demonstrations in military order; the organisation of squads of stewards which assume sole responsibility for order at meetings. The Fascists and Nazis went on to use such organisations to provoke riots and street-fighting; other parties were so placed that they must either seem ineffectual or reply in kind, and both lines of action were disastrous to electoral democracy.

Resistance to Fascism failed in Italy and Germany partly because there was tacit sympathy between police and army on the one side, the Fascists on the other: this was what Fascists and Nazis wished the public to believe, and unfortunately it was in substance true. In such circumstances, free elections are in the end impossible: but if police and army are loyal to the idea of a state founded on consent, the control of para-military organisations is not difficult. Party armies are amateurish at best, and cannot stand against professionals acting in earnest. Similarly, it is easy to defeat attempts by parties to replace the police by their own squads of stewards and strong-arm men if the official police are adequately financed and resolutely led, and have sufficient professional pride to regard with disgust the efforts of self-appointed 'auxiliaries'.

These principles of control are better understood now than in the days of the Ulster Volunteers and the Irish Volunteers, or of Mussolini's *squadristi* and Hitler's first 'storm-troopers'. Any competent government can now stop threats of this kind before they become serious: the question at present is whether governments have become so cautious that they discourage all public demonstrations of party strength lest they become a threat to public order. It is not easy to draw the line between defence of public order against a show of force through numbers, and defence of the existing government against a rising party which wishes to replace it. Opposition, even Communist opposition, in Western countries has for some time been very docile; the problem of control of mass parties following 'charismatic' leaders is one that principally troubles 'colonial' governments during the process of transferring power to local people. To introduce elections in a traditional society involves also the introduction of new mass organisations: the process by which such organisations are created is more delicate and dangerous than the electoral process itself. The British have on the whole been judicious (or fortunate) in India, the Gold Coast and Nigeria; but elsewhere—in Malaya for instance and in Kenya—nascent political parties have attempted to establish themselves by violence directed largely against their own countrymen, and have been checked by armed forces brought in from outside.

3. Polling-Day

All these questions come to a head on polling-day, which may be a serious test of police organisation if the public is excitable and party leaders are reckless. On the whole, elections in the West are so much a matter of course that the risk of disorder is very small: in countries where elections are new they are generally treated with great respect, and the public itself maintains good order as an indication of its political maturity. But it is not difficult to distort the results of an election, or even to wreck it completely, by organised violence: quite a small number of people, working to a common plan, can create by pre-arranged outbreaks an atmosphere of general uneasiness, and the position may deteriorate quickly if the election is closely contested.

To handle such dangers is a matter of police tactics rather than of political science. To the layman the secrets of success appear to be adequate information, adequate communications, and adequate concentration of force. It is usual to post a policeman in or near each polling station, as a symbol of authority and an immediate support for the presiding officer. But one man is of little value in a crisis unless he can summon support quickly, and effective control depends on the mobility of police reserves. If they are known to be at hand, the risk of violence is greatly reduced.

It may in certain circumstances be useful to spread a general election over several days, so that limited police reserves can be used successively in different parts of the country, and this may also (as was suggested in Chapter XIV) be useful in deploying limited resources of trained clerks. This idea of a general election spread over a period is sanctioned by a British tradition ended only in 1918, and it is hard to see any objection to it in principle. It is, however, best to avoid it, if possible, in countries where there are adequate mass communications, because the progress of the election in the first constituencies to poll becomes known throughout the country, and may affect the voters elsewhere: *how* it affects them is difficult to say—some may climb on the 'bandwagon' of the winners, others may see a new danger and vote against it—but the mere fact that some constituencies poll first may lead to endless arguments. These difficulties might be met by delaying the count, or the announcement of results, for the first constituencies to poll: but such a remedy creates other problems.

4. *Conclusion.*

What has been said above is directed mainly to the question of how public force may be used to exclude private force from intervention in elections. Everyone knows that public force may itself be a danger to freedom: if public force is identified by public opinion with the government in power, the government's claim that it is using force to maintain order will in itself be a threat to its opponents. In the last resort, therefore, the system of free elections depends on a certain separation of powers between administrators (or policemen) and politicians: there must be some public sense that police and administration serve the public, not the party leaders.

The Marxist view of the situation is that this cannot happen, and that the pretence that it can happen is a mere fraud. The doctrine of Marxist elections, in which the choice is between voting for the government and seeking to subvert the regime, follows consistently enough from these premises. The theorists of free elections would answer that a class view of society is a limited view: class domination exists and is important, but the existence of strong semi-independent groups within society is also important, and the idea of established professions of administrators, soldiers and policemen partly independent of the politicians is no more paradoxical than the idea of professions of doctors, lawyers, scientists and engineers, exercising within their own spheres great power subject to public responsibility. The debate between these two points of view is too complex for serious discussion here: all that need be said is that the effective organisation of free elections presupposes the tradition of a public service independent within its own professional sphere.

CHAPTER XVIII

Corrupt Practices

1. *Introductory*

The characteristic complaint about popular elections until late in the nineteenth century was that they led to the sale of votes: that is to say, to individual transactions between poor men who had votes and rich men who wanted seats. Individual corruption of this kind is almost extinct in Western societies. This is due partly to the large size of modern electorates, partly to a tacit bargain between competing parties. Parties agree that on the whole the purchase of individual votes is expensive and embarrassing, and therefore discourage zealots anxious to compete in this sort of auction. But legislation on corrupt practices also played a considerable part in the transition from ancient to modern elections, and there is a repertoire of legal provisions to be taken over by any new electoral system. In the last resort, the efficacy of these rules depends on public opinion and on party support, but good rules effectively enforced may give a twist to events which is important if other forces are evenly balanced.

Money may also be applied to influence individuals at other points in the system: for instance, by bribing clerks in compiling the register: by payments to individuals for candidatures designed only to embarrass opponents, or for withdrawal from the contest; by influence on the process of supervising the poll and counting the votes. A comprehensive electoral code naturally forbids the offer of payment or any other consideration by a candidate to another candidate or to any official concerned with the election. The voter is, however, the easiest and most important point of attack, and this primarily concerns us here.

2. *Control of expenditure*

The most important British discovery in this sphere has been the invention of the post of electoral agent and the introduction of control over a candidate's expenses through accounts presented by the agent. Most other Western systems are now as free from corrupt practices as is the British system; nevertheless, the device of accounting through an agent is the neatest technical method of control, and it has been widely copied in countries influenced by British practice.

Candidates in Britain have appointed agents from time immemorial, but till the middle of the nineteenth century they were employed principally to 'see to the register' and to make payments about which the candidate preferred to know nothing. It was not until 1883 that the appointment of an agent was made compulsory. At the same time, it was laid down that the candidate must not during the election period incur any expenses of certain specified kinds except through his agent, and that the agent must submit full accounts to the returning officer within a limited period after the declaration of the poll. Moreover, a limit was set to the amount which the agent might legally spend on behalf of his candidate.

The rule is that when nominated a candidate must appoint an agent (he may appoint himself if he wishes), and that thereafter no expenditure is to be incurred for his campaign except through his agent. The agents are usually the local party organisers of the main parties concerned, and are active between elections in association with a multitude of party committees: but when the candidate is nominated and his agent is appointed, these party organisations formally cease to exist, so that there can be no local source of campaign expenditure except the agent himself.

The agent's permissible expenditure is limited to a sum depending on the number of electors, with a small allowance for the candidate's personal expenses. At present, the allowance is £450 plus three-halfpence per elector in urban constituencies and twopence for each elector in the country, with £100 for the personal expenses of the candidate: this amounts to £925 in an urban constituency of 60,000 electors and £1,050 in a rural constituency of the same size. In present circumstances this is not a large sum of money (some county elections in the eighteenth and early nineteenth centuries are said to have cost each candidate over £100,000 at prices then current), and it limits the campaign to the bare minimum of posters, loud-speaker cars, and small meetings. Perhaps, however, the low limit is to some extent welcome to the local branches of all parties alike, because it prevents excessive competition in raising party funds.

The agent's accounts must be presented within thirty-five days after the day on which the result of the election is declared, and must include details of specific items of expenditure. The accounts are checked, assembled nationally, and published, so that it is possible to see what has been spent by each party on local campaigns. For the 1955 election this amounted to about £458,000 for the Conservatives and £378,000 for the Labour Party: this does not include any expenditure by party headquarters on national campaigns, a matter outside the scope of this sort of control, except in so far as it can be allocated to individual constituencies, as for instance in the cost of 'literature' produced centrally for local distribution.

The system has certain difficulties: for instance, all expenditure during the campaign must be accounted for, but the 'campaign' begins before nomination day, that is to say, before the agent has been appointed, and it is not at all easy to say as a matter of law when it does begin. This is, however, a legal gap which could be closed if it became serious; and the advantages of the system greatly outweigh its demerits. One of the difficulties in repressing corruption is that it is always more difficult to prove an intention than to prove an act: there can be no direct evidence about states of mind, and sufficient doubt can be sown by the defence to make conviction dangerous. Hence the most effective way to attack corruption is not by increasing penalties for the offence itself, but by specifying rules of a formal kind which are to be observed. Breach of these rules is not in itself evidence of corruption: but the rules are defended by the law as part of a general system of protection against corruption.

In other words, it is easier to prosecute for technical offences than for substantive offences. Almost all electoral codes contain formal rules about expenditure which is prohibited irrespective of intention. The system of electoral agents is the most comprehensive possible arrangement of this type. Under it, it becomes an offence for anyone to spend any money locally in support of a candidate except through the agent, and for the agent to spend any money for which he does not account, or to spend money above the permitted amount. That is to say, it is necessary only to prove the relatively simple proposition that money has been spent, not the obscure proposition that it has been spent corruptly: observation and control by public authorities, or by one party watching another, is immensely simplified.

Such technical offences, if isolated, are relatively venial: they are 'illegal practices', not 'corrupt practices', and they are not penalised by disfranchisement or by disqualification for membership. But the penalties, in cash and in public esteem, are severe enough to be effective.

3. Improper expenditure

Even where this system of accounting is not used, electoral codes specify in considerable detail the ways in which money is not to be spent: and there are similar details in British law, deriving largely from an earlier period.

It need scarcely be said that it is a corrupt practice to offer an elector a sum of money, a job or other valuable consideration in reward for voting one way or another. This is an offence, whether the voter is in fact corrupted or not.

Naturally, cautious agents preferred to evade rather than to break the law: hence a number of topics famous in parliamentary history.

It is possible to pay electors during the campaign for assistance other than assistance by their votes: for instance, as bandsmen in processions, as clerks in committee rooms, as stewards at meetings, and so on. A rich candidate can disburse a good deal of money in this way, so as to surround himself with henchmen wearing the party colours, about whose votes he need not trouble to enquire. It is hard to strike at this directly except by limiting the number of party employees: limitation through a specified allowance for electoral expenditure is much simpler.

Similarly with the traditional custom of 'treating'. Public opinion in a constituency might in the old days virtually compel the candidates to open the public-houses to their supporters: some houses might be for the Blues, others for the Yellows, and drink flowed freely. A man might drink Blue beer and vote Yellow: probably this was rare, and in some sense free beer paid for votes. But corrupt intent could never be proved in a court of law, and no remedy was possible (when the parties in effect finally agreed on 'disarmament') except complete prohibition of all treating during the election period. This had advantages also from the point of view of public order: some countries for this reason stop all public sale of alcohol on polling day.

Rather different problems arose out of the offer of inducements not easy to measure financially and not directly related to an election: to purchase or not to purchase at a particular shop, to alter one way or the other the terms of a bargain about lands, a house or goods, even to exclude from a particular religious community (there is still trouble in many countries about the influence of the preacher over his flock). British law refers in wide terms to 'undue influence', 'temporal or spiritual', but such provisions are easy to evade, and the only effective checks are the secret ballot, the growth in the size of electorates, and the readiness of opposing party organisations to bring cases before the public.

These traditional practices have dwindled in the twentieth century, and the only new problem is that of the use of cars in elections. In a sense, this is a matter for the next chapter, since it is suggested that wealthy parties gain an advantage through their resources in transport without any direct bribery of individuals: but the question is so much concerned with local arrangements in each constitioncy that it is convenient to introduce it here. Perhaps in the early days of the motor-car it was a form of bribery to offer voters a ride: eventually ownership of cars may be so widespread that it is unnecessary for the parties to organise transport. But Britain and other Western countries are in an intermediate stage; the problem for the parties in a close-fought election is to bring out the vote, and it may be a real advantage to be able to send cars for old people, invalids, cripples and voters in out-lying parts of the constituency. Cars are of course used for other voters too; anyone who is at hand will take a lift to the poll (generally only in a car which bears the right colours), and a supply of cars is useful in bringing out laggard voters from their firesides in the evening. It is not possible to assess accurately how the use of cars affects voting: but certainly lack of cars worries parties which do not possess them.

Hence the attempt in the Representation of the People Act of 1948 to restore the balance by limiting the use of cars to a number proportionate to the size of the electorate (one for every 2,500 in the towns, for every 1,500 in the country), and by specifying that all cars used by the parties on election day must be registered for the purpose. These rules have not proved very easy to interpret, since they cannot prevent a man from giving his neighbours a lift when he is going to vote (as long as he does not display party colours), they have been quite unimportant in British elections since 1948, and the extension of car ownership is gradually rendering them obsolete. But the use of cars may still be important in countries of greater distances and less wealth. It is reported that in the Lebanon elections of 1957 the price of taxis was bid up to £30 a day, by competition between the parties; there was even an allegation in Singapore that a candidate 'employed women of doubtful virtue to ride in election cars to tempt men to the polls'.

It has never been the fashion to attempt to repress corruption by imprisonment or even by heavy fines. Minor cases of corruption or illegality without proof of corrupt intent may be dealt with by small routine penalties: but public opinion is unlikely to support the imposition of ordinary criminal penalties except in cases which threaten public order. Hence the tendency in dealing with corruption is to look for punishments that fit the crime. These are easy to find: not always easy to assess.

There are three categories:—

(a) *Effect on the elections.* It is natural to provide that if a successful candidate is proved to have acted corruptly his election should be invalid. This may mean *either* that the candidate with the next highest vote is declared elected, *or* that the whole election in that constituency is void and must be repeated. The choice of penalty may be affected to some extent by the system of voting: for instance, if there is a system of P.R. in multi-member constituencies it may cause disproportionate inconvenience to insist on a new election in a large constituency because one of a number of successful candidates is proved to have acted corruptly, unless it is shown that his action has benefited his list as a whole.

In practice, it often happens that corruption, once begun, has proved infectious, and that all the candidates are guilty in some degree; in that case clearly the election must be repeated.

It may sometimes be possible to prove the corruption of individual voters but not to bring the offence home to any of the candidates, in a personal sense: in that case, it is natural to deduct the corrupt votes, leaving the election to stand without them.

(b) *Effect on the voters.* It was the practice in England before the 1832 Reform Act for the House of Commons to disfranchise a borough proved guilty of persistent corruption by merging it in the county in which it lay, and sometimes by bestowing its seat or seats elsewhere. This belongs to the system of the representation of communities rather than of individuals, and there are some parts of the world where it may still be relevant: but it would be out of place in most countries. The alternative to it is the disfranchisement of individuals proved guilty of corruption; either permanent loss of rights, or disfranchisement for a period thought to be proportionate to the offence.

(c) *Effect on the candidate.* A candidate who has acted corruptly or who has knowingly permitted others to act corruptly on his behalf can reasonably be penalised by disfranchisement. But from the politician's point of view the penalty of disqualification for candidature is a more serious one. It is important that the law should provide disqualification for candidature, not disqualification for election: the latter may permit a corrupt but popular politician to stand again, win a majority, and throw on his opponents the onus of excluding him from the elected assembly. Disqualification may be temporary or permanent, in one constituency or in all constituencies.

In all three categories the law may prescribe a sentence which follows automatically upon conviction, or it may leave discretion to the judge. There is a great deal to be said for automatic sentences, since they lessen the burden upon a judge acting in a controversial matter of party politics: but they are only possible if public opinion considers the legal sentence appropriate to the offence—otherwise it will be hard to secure conviction. In almost all systems offences fall into the two categories referred to earlier, substantive and technical. It may often be possible to secure conviction and a mild penalty for a technical offence when public opinion is not strong enough to support prosecution on a graver charge and to provide evidence. As a French scholar, a judge of the Conseil d'Etat, the administrative court which supervises procedure, in colonial and local elections, wrote recently, judges ought to take a severe rather than a lenient view of such matters of form: it is their only means of educating politicians and people in the true doctrine, that 'une élection n'est ni une farce, ni une fête, ni un match de catch, mais une opération déterminante pour la vie des sociétés,'[1] (An election is not a joke, nor a public holiday, nor a game of rounders, but a way of making decisions vital to the life of society.)

---

[1] André Holleaux in the *Revue Juridique et Politique de l'Union Française*, January-March, 1956, at p. 46.

CHAPTER XIX

Money in Elections

1. *The Problem*

Free elections, we have seen, are elections in which each voter has the opportunity—an equal opportunity—to express consent in the light of his own opinions and sentiments. Intimidation is one form of attack on this independence, bribery is another form, as dangerous though at first sight less repulsive. But individual corruption of the older type has virtually died out in Western societies; the impact of money on elections now assumes different forms.

The dilemma is in principle a simple one. Free elections depend on free communications: the law must defend the right of every citizen to put his view before the electorate by any means consistent with public order and with the protection of individuals against malicious personal attacks. But mass communication is very expensive; complete freedom of communication gives the advantage to rich men and rich parties, and therefore tends to a breach of equality. The extreme case is that in which the regime as monopolist of power and wealth asserts a monopoly of all forms of mass communication, and attempts to 'condition' its people, by deciding what political information and arguments are to reach them and what is to be the general 'tone' of discussion about matters which seem at first sight politically neutral. We can recognise this as 'unfreedom': the situation is more puzzling when the balance is more even, and there has been much discussion both of the extent to which money does in fact influence elections through propaganda, and of the methods by which that influence might be limited in the interest of equality, without prejudice to freedom of speech.

The situation is puzzling but not at present alarming. There is plenty of evidence that the public is not as simple as is sometimes thought, and that the trend of opinion often runs counter to the main stream of propaganda. Republican domination of the press and the air in America, Conservative predominance in British newspapers have not prevented strong swings of opinion against Republican and Conservative governments and against the 'establishment' in general on many occasions in the last generation. In a free country people talk about what they read and hear, and if things are not going well for them as individuals they talk rudely and critically. It is an assertion of personal independence, a hobby of popular sages in public bars, drug stores and

159

cafés, to disbelieve what those in power say about the facts and to sneer at their exhortations. Even under totalitarian regimes the response to continued exhortation is often negative; and the Western public are pretty sceptical about what they 'see in the papers'.

On the other hand, this scepticism is merely destructive unless the public are offered alternative views of the situation between which to choose. A single dissenting newspaper or a limited amount of opposition time on the air may be disproportionately important because it offers a rallying point and a coherent view of the situation to people who would otherwise be left to their own limited and scattered resources of experience. It may be that if the control of mass communications is divided 80/20 rather than 50/50, this disproportion makes less difference than might be expected: but the argument cannot be taken further, to prove that monopoly, or near monopoly, is unimportant.

Apart from this, dominance not amounting to monopoly may be more important in creating tone and atmosphere than it is in affecting the immediate decision between parties. The Democratic party suffers less electorally than might be expected from its relative poverty: but Democratic and Republican politicians alike work within the atmosphere described vaguely as the 'American way of life', an atmosphere created largely by the commercial press, cinema, radio and television, as much through advertisements as through news features, fiction and editorials. Similarly in Britain, the Labour Party is not gravely handicapped because the circulation of Labour daily papers is relatively small: but a mass-circulation Labour paper looks much the same as a mass circulation Conservative paper, the focus of public interest shifts irrespective of party alignments, and there are changing moods of opinion which affect both parties alike. It is in theory possible for rich men to influence these trends of opinion through power over mass communications: little research has been done on the extent of this influence, but there have been a number of conspicuous failures, and the general impression is that those who succeed commercially do so by gauging the atmosphere of opinion, not by creating it.

In attempting to limit the influence of money in elections, there are four keys points—the local campaign in the constituencies, the control of national party funds, the press, the use of broadcast radio and television.

2. The Local Campaign

The problem is most easy to tackle in the constituencies, and there are two well-established methods which complement one another.

(a) *Limitation of expenditure by candidates.* In Chapter XVIII we referred to the imposition of limits on the amount to be spent by a candidate during the period of his campaign. This was introduced primarily to combat corruption: but it has the incidental advantage that it equalises poor and wealthy candidates, poor and wealthy party organisations. If each party organisation watches the others, it is relatively easy to enforce strict accounting for expenditure within a defined area, and it is also possible to make some assessment of what a 'reasonable' limit of expenditure would be.

There are, however, two difficulties which always cause trouble. One is that it is possible to limit expenditure during the campaign, defined in a fairly narrow sense, but it is not possible to limit all expenditure in the constituency. The life of a constituency is unified and continuous and rich men there who wish to spend money on public purposes cannot be prevented from doing so: it is virtually impossible to draw a line between disinterested benevolence and benevolence which improves the chances of a particular organisation or individual.

The other difficulty is that of separating the constituency campaign from the national campaign. British electoral law provides that any expenditure designed to assist the candidature of an individual must be included in his agent's accounts. The party organisations and the national party press are therefore scrupulous in avoiding direct support for individual candidates; yet their advocacy of the party and its policy is bound to help individuals indirectly, is indeed designed to do so, and so are their decisions about what speeches and events in the constituencies to report as news.

(b) *State assistance to candidates*. Perhaps for these reasons, British practice has not been widely copied. But the same effect of equalisation (though not of control) can be secured if the state helps all candidates alike to bear the cost of their campaigns. There must, however, be some limit to the state's liability: if it were prepared to subsidise all candidates it would incur unlimited expense and would confuse the process of elections by multiplying candidates. Hence such provisions as the £150 deposit subject to forfeiture, in Britain (though here the state gives little assistance apart from free postage for one communication to all voters); in France, the rule that candidates or lists not securing $2\frac{1}{2}\%$ of the votes in a constituency forfeit all state assistance, and forfeit some assistance if they do not reach 5%. [1]

So far as the writer knows, state assistance is nowhere given in the form of a cash grant to be spent freely subject to the presentation of accounts. The usual practice is to give assistance in a number of specified ways, sometimes by reimbursements of charges incurred by candidates, more frequently by direct state expenditure on their behalf. The most common forms are: printing of posters and their display on official

[1] There is also a small deposit.

sites (sometimes accompanied by the prohibition of all other electoral posters): printing of a specified amount of electoral material and its distribution to electors through the post without cost to candidates; provision of halls for public meetings (particularly in schools): provision of free petrol or assistance in other ways with travelling expenses.

Perhaps one reason why measures of limitation and subvention are acceptable and are fairly common is that they tend to strengthen centralisation within political parties, and at the same time to transfer part of the cost of running them from party supporters to the taxpayer. If a constituency is a closely-knit community, such measures will not much affect the influence of rich men within it, since their money counts in many ways outside the short period of the electoral campaign. But they do reduce the margin between rich and poor in electoral districts which have no internal unity. Subventions help all parties alike, but decrease the relative importance of local organisation, since little is to be gained in the campaign by raising money locally. Limitation of expenses in the constituencies limits the scope of local campaigns, however financed, but leaves the field open for the extension of national campaigns. The next question is therefore whether anything can be done (or should be done) to limit the influence of money at that level.

3. *Party funds*

There is no topic more popular among party politicians than that of the sources from which other parties draw their money, but agreement between them on control is unlikely, and even if it were politically possible, effective control would be difficult to devise.

There are few who think it practicable to limit the amount of money which might be raised and spent by a political party. There is no basis for reckoning what expenditure would be 'reasonable': even if there were, a limit could not be enforced except by thorough police supervision and much litigation. Secrecy in expenditure at the national level is relatively easy, much easier than within a local constituency where important transactions quickly become known. It is also easy to evade practically any legal definition: how can one prevent individuals from spending money on objects which are not exactly the objects of any political party but happen to resemble those of one party in some respects? It is relevant to quote the example of Messrs. Tate and Lyle, great sugar growers and manufacturers, who launched a campaign of their own against the nationalisation of sugar just before the British election of 1950: this coincided with the objects of the Conservative Party, but it was decided judicially that it was a question of advertising designed to protect the commercial interests of the company, not on political purposes. There is no British law about central party funds, and this case was one about income-tax: but it illustrates how difficult it is to draw enforceable lines between contributions to party funds, independent expenditure in support of a party, and independent expenditure on private objects which partly coincide with those of a party.

There are two alternatives to control: one is to limit the amount which any individual or firm may subscribe to a party organisation, the other is to require the publication of party accounts. The former was introduced in the U.S.A. by the Hatch Act of 1940, and has been observed quite scrupulously in a formal sense: no firm or individual may give more than $5,000 to a party organisation in any one year. But the practical efforts have been negligible. A party can evade the law by multiplying itself in various subsidiary organisations, an individual can evade it by multiplying himself through his family, his friends and his associated firms.

The idea of publicity for party accounts is more promising, perhaps the only promising approach to this difficult question. Its advantage is that once established it is to some extent self-enforcing. No police force, no judicial system can verify the accuracy of party accounts: but if accounts of some sort, in some official form, are published by all parties, the matter is thrown open to debate. At present, if a party maintains complete secrecy about its funds, there is no admitted evidence from which to begin discussion about how it is financed; once accounts are available, even in a simple form, other parties are given a starting-point for analysis and criticism, and it is then easier for the public to form a sensible opinion because it hears both sides of the story. Publicity for party accounts cannot stop secret expenditure on political objects, but it can do something to control it, if conditions are otherwise favourable.

4. *The Press*

It is perhaps easiest to approach the question of political campaigning in the press by distinguishing two types of journal; the distinction is not always clear in practice, but it indicates what the points at issue are. Some journals are primarily partisan: they are sponsored by a political group or party to further its aims, and they are managed by people who are primarily politicians. Others are primarily commercial enterprises, designed at one time to make a profit by selling reading matter to the public, now maintained primarily to sell a public to advertisers by selling advertising space in a journal with a big circulation. An enterprise of this sort can only continue if it makes a profit, and its success depends not on influencing public opinion but on gauging accurately what the public wants.

The category of political journals raises no special problems. A rich party can afford to spend more money in this way than can a poor one, but expenditure on printed matter is unimportant unless it secures readers. Political journals in the strict sense are read mainly by the party faithful; they are important in the affairs of the party, but have little direct effect on the public. Political reading-matter intended for the public (whether sold or given away) is not very important unless the public actually wants to have it.

It is this fact which gives extreme importance to the position of the commercial press. In one sense, commercial management of the press is a security for freedom, because it is safer to trust those who are trying to please the public than those who are trying to persuade it. But costs of production and distribution, and the character of the market for advertising space, diminish the effect of commercial competition in giving variety and freedom of choice, because journals are concentrated in the hands of a few large enterprises: and it is a temptation (rarely resisted) for the proprietors of these enterprises to seek to use them politically. The political ambitions of newspaper magnates are still limited by commercial competition: they must respond quickly to a fall in circulation, and it is a delicate exercise in the assessment of public taste to mix politics with news and entertainment in a proportion which does not break the market. The public can thus defend itself against the magnates, if they become bores; a commercial press, with all its faults, fits a system of free elections better than does a controlled press. But its faults are grave, and no hopeful expedients have been devised for correcting them.

Some experiments have been made in Western countries in the management of newspapers such as *The Times*, *The Manchester Guardian*, *The Observer* and *Le Monde*, under trusts which prevent the sale of the enterprise in the open market and impose some of the obligations of a public utility on its proprietors. But these papers are not in any sense 'nationalised', nor are they insulated from the effects of the market or from the personal prejudices of their owners and editors. Indeed, no one in the West believes that nationalisation, even under independent public corporations, would help to solve the problem. A limited experiment in France after the liberation was not at all successful.

The nationalised press of Russia and other Communist countries is in principle put 'at the disposal of the working people and their organisations'. This constitutional provision is not wholly fraudulent: such a press does serve (when the government pleases) to give an outlet for individual opinions and grievances. But the main objects of a free press are defeated because it is a grave crime to organise complaints by joint action except under the aegis of the regime, and there can therefore be no campaigns except official campaigns: and because such journals exist independently of a market, and are therefore free from any obligation to pay heed to public interests and tastes.

Various other devices have been tried, with limited success. Freedom of the press involves freedom of editorial policy, subject only to limitations on incitement to violence and sabotage and on the sale of pornography: but it is not incompatible with this freedom to restrict attacks on individuals and mis-statements of fact. In Britain laws of libel and of Parliamentary privilege limit fairly closely the scope of personal attacks on individuals. The individual is not so effectively protected by the law in France and in the U.S.A.: but the former gives by law the right of contradiction, with space and prominence equivalent to that of the original statement, in the unlikely event of a successful action for libel. On the whole, this right to reply to personal, as distinct from political, attacks is accepted in principle by the Western press, and it is to some extent enforced by the professional standards of good journalism. Similarly, if a newspaper sells advertising space to one party or interest to state its case, it recognises some obligation, in the name of free enterprise, to sell equivalent space to any other organisation at the same price—if it can pay for it. But these limits of law and professional ethics are much less significant than the attitude of the public; only the public can resist biassed editorial comment and 'angled' news, and it becomes more difficult for it to do so as its choice of journals decreases.

5. Sound Radio and Television

It was from the first necessary to exercise some public control over broadcasting, because uncontrolled use of frequencies would make all effective broadcasting impossible. Control may be exercised through a government department or commission supervising stations which operate commercially; or through a licensed public corporation: or through direct operation by a government department; or by a combination of these. In any event, the issues arise about the political uses of a publicly-controlled medium and cannot be evaded. Almost everywhere, the inference is drawn from public control that the government can in the last resort use any or all broadcasting stations to announce matters of national importance. But this reserve power is of little day-to-day importance, because important announcements are 'news', and radio stations are as eager as newspapers to give them publicity. Ordinary practice varies within a very wide range, from almost free commercial operation to concentration of all effort on objects indicated by the regime.

The lightest possible form of control is the requirement that if a commercial station rents time on the air to one organisation, it should rent an equivalent amount of time, at an equivalent listening hour, at the same price, to any other organisation which wishes to join issue. This is common American practice: it biasses matters in favour of rich organisations, so that in presidential elections the Republicans usually secure much more time on the air than do the Democrats. But the big American broadcasting organisations go a good deal beyond their legal obligations to the Federal Communications Commission, and make time available without cost for debates on major issues of policy; to put it at the lowest, this is good business because it attracts listeners.

In the centre of the scale, is the rather elaborate code worked out by the B.B.C. in discussion (and often in violent disagreement) with the main political parties during the period when it held a monopoly of British broadcasting. (The French state radio system faces similar problems). At all times some periods are made available free of charge for 'party political broadcasts': during elections the number of such broadcasts is greatly increased, and the parties treat them as a very important part of the campaign. They certainly reach enormous audiences, though there is not much evidence that the audiences are affected in their opinions, one way or the other.

The B.B.C. system aims at extreme fairness, but encounters two difficulties of principle. One is that of deciding which parties to recognise and how to allocate the available time between them. At present, there are no parties in Britain which are outside the pale as illegal organisations: the Communist Party (and presumably a Fascist Party, should one become substantial) are recognised as eligible, and so are the small Nationalist Parties of Scotland and Wales. But clearly not all parties can be given equal time: if time on the air is not to be rationed by the purse it must be rationed in some other way. As a starting-point, it is agreed that the two main parties, which contest practically all constituencies should rank equally. But what about the minor parties? Party membership is a useless criterion, because different parties are differently organised, and in any case figures could easily be falsified. Seats in the House of Commons may serve as a criterion and are commonly so used. But this may exaggerate somewhat the time given to small parties (in practice, the Liberal Party) which do have seats in the House, at the expense of those which have not yet got so far. Another measure in use, especially at election times, is that of the number of candidates nominated: but this is open to the objection that time on the air can be 'bought' by running additional candidates. Suppose that the B.B.C. names a minimum number of candidates which qualifies a party to broadcast: say thirty candidates for half an hour on the air, and so *pro rata*. If a party (say a small nationalist party) thinks it sound on other grounds to run twenty-five candidates, then it may well stake five more deposits, £750 (which can partly be covered by insurance), in order to buy half an hour in which to talk to an audience of perhaps ten million people. It would reduce this temptation if time were allocated on the basis of votes polled at the preceding general election, but an election in single-member constituencies may not give a very accurate picture of party strength for the whole country. In any case, what logical ground is there for allocating time in which to express views on the basis of those convinced in different circumstances, perhaps by different views, some time before? The best one can say is that by combining these forms of measurement, and by hard bargaining between parties, a rationing system has been evolved which gives some opportunity to all important bodies of political opinion.

But what is 'political' opinion? The other difficulty facing the B.B.C. as a public body is that in the course of its ordinary programmes—discussions, variety, plays, as well as news—someone may express an opinion which some political party regards as hostile to itself. It then demands the right of reply, and in default of agreement denounces the B.B.C. for political bias.

The B.B.C. defends itself in various ways. In the first place, it attempts to draw a distinction between 'political' and 'party political', which is rather like the distinction between 'religion' and 'sectarian religion' drawn in English state schools. There is a demand for broadcasters who can talk about matters of public interest without identifying themselves with any organised party, a demand which works in two directions: if such broadcasters talk badly they make public issues boring; if they succeed, they contribute to the impression (already quite strong in Western countries) that political parties are led by people who evade the most important issues in their attempt to catch votes. Public patronage of 'non-party politics' reflects on the status of political parties, just as public patronage of 'non-sectarian religion' (which began in 1871) reflected on, and in the end lowered, the status of religious sects.

Secondly, it attempts to hold the balance between opposing views about any question which can conceivably be said to have two sides to it. A debate or quiz or brains-trust often makes good broadcasting, and it also helps the B.B.C. to solve the problem of balance.

Thirdly, it may think it wisest to evade certain issues altogether. This is sometimes a matter of instructions from the government, for instance over the very controversial question whether it is bad for the prestige of the House of Commons that an issue should be discussed publicly on the air shortly before a debate in Parliament. Back-bench M.P.s of all parties dislike such B.B.C. discussions: they have great difficulty in finding the opportunity to express their views in the House, why should other people be given priority to express their views to the nation? The B.B.C. first limited itself by agreement with the parties, then insisted on a formal directive from the government about its course of action. On many other matters it exercises self-censorship, perhaps even without much internal discussion, because of the risk of attracting criticism from the parties. Its policy, for instance, in gathering and reporting foreign news which has a bearing on British policy is certainly less enterprising than that of first-class periodicals.

This discussion has led us some way from elections, and this is inevitable, because there can be no sharp lines of distinction between the electoral period and the rest of political life, between party propaganda and other forms of public discussion. The difficulties of the B.B.C. arise from the nature of the problem, not from the personalities of its successive Directors-General. There is something paradoxical about the notion that those in power should provide equal facilities for all those who seek to exclude them from power by persuading the electorate to change its mind, and it is not easy to work out such a doctrine consistently in practice. Nevertheless, the experience of Western countries is that, in this as in so many other respects, the system of free elections can be made to work, not without much groaning and travail, but at least better than any of the alternatives which confront it.

CHAPTER XX

Conclusion: the Pathology of Elections

1. *Introductory*

There is no one right way of conducting elections, but there are a number of ways which are clearly wrong: wrong in the logical sense that they apply the machinery of elections to negate the declared objects of the machinery. This sometimes happens because electoral systems are introduced in conditions quite unsuitable for them, and they are therefore distorted by social forces in a way which no one ever intended: sometimes because dominant regimes deliberately take refuge in 'newspeak' and 'double-think', and use the formula of free elections to disguise a situation in which no free choice is offered; sometimes perhaps, because of purely administrative mistakes, failures to set up electoral machinery suitable to the society within which it is to operate.

These distortions are not necessarily 'wrong' in a moral sense; they may not arise through anyone's fault, they may even be justifiable socially, in the sense that in given circumstances any other procedure would lead to riots, killings, civil war and self-destruction of society. Nor are they marked off from free elections as black from white. No elections can realise perfect freedom: almost any use of the notion of election makes some use of the idea of freedom. But it seems fair to talk of pathology, because there is a recognisable norm and there are different patterns of departure from it. These may be summarised as muddled elections, stolen elections, made elections, and elections by acclamation.

2. *Muddled elections*

We have referred several times in earlier chapters to the need for parties as an organising factor in elections. Theorists in the eighteenth century thought of elections as the choice by voters of individuals to act for them in a representative assembly: the organisation of the assembly was something quite separate from the organisation of the electorate, and at both levels parties were judged to be evil because they encouraged faction. The nineteenth century learnt better from longer experience; it became clear that a large assembly must be organised by someone in order to do business at all. If it were organised by a government or by a single clique it became a rubber stamp in their hands; freedom of debate could be combined with order only if there were several organised 'caucuses' or legislative parties. Once this was realised, it followed that there must also be electoral parties, to establish some connection between public opinion and the cliques or caucuses in the legislature: party became respectable, even where it did not effectively exist.

This is still the view generally held. The elector cannot be offered a choice on national questions unless there are national parties; his choice will not be effective unless each of the parties which solicit his vote and which act in the assembly coheres strongly and obeys some consistent set of internal rules. Elections will be 'muddled' if there are no effective electoral parties, or if parties in the assembly go their own way regardless of the electorate. 'Muddle' is likely to lead either to irresolute government or to resolute government distrusted by the people because not linked to them by choice.

There is some truth in this view, but the theory must not be taken too seriously. Human affairs are always in a state of muddle; muddled politics are not the worst sort of politics; and muddles often have a curious stability of their own. The most that should be said is that in certain circumstances a clear decision is necessary and that muddle is then a source of danger, in other circumstances it is an escape from dangerous internal divisions. It is doubtless beyond human ingenuity to plan a system dependable for both purposes.

3. *Stolen elections*

By a 'stolen' election we mean here one in which inducements of individual advantage are more important in determining votes than either considerations affecting the voter's group or class or party as a whole, or considerations about the general public interest, or both together. The offer of bribes to voters and officials is in practice always mixed up with threats to withhold benefits already enjoyed, and corruption is therefore not far from intimidation. But the tone of such situations is that of inducement rather than repression: an elector is at least free to sell his vote. To quote a comment on the 1957 elections in the Lebanon: 'We've never had such free elections. No pressure at all. There's money for anyone who wants to sell his vote, and anyone who wants to follow his conscience can do that too'. Stolen elections, interpreted in this sense, have a history long enough to lend them a certain dignity. They have had their laureates, Hogarth and Rowlandson, Dickens and 'Mr. Dooley'; great men have reached high office through corrupt management of elections from the days of Pym and Hampden, Fox and Pitt, to those of Mr. Gladstone and Abraham Lincoln. Stolen elections have this place in the history of democracy because they enabled electoral practice to adapt itself to the prevailing social system through innumerable ties of personal interest, and yet left open opportunities for free debate, for endless local variety, and in the end for reform. But even Burke in defending the curious patchwork of the old English electoral system did not defend corruption: corruption is not always disastrous to the state, but it is in itself bad; and it is not wise to introduce elections at all if they are likely to become radically corrupt.

There is less risk of corruption under universal suffrage than with very small electorates, because mass propaganda is cheaper than mass bribery, and perhaps almost as effective. But the risk is always present in a society the structure of which contradicts the assumptions of a system of free elections. Such a system presupposes the possibility of individual decision by at least some voters, and the free organisation of parties and other groups to mobilise votes behind leaders and policies. Corruption is therefore probable if elections are introduced in a situation in which society is organised hierarchically on the basis of some kind of 'feudal' leadership, or in groups like African tribes or Arab families and religious orders, which cohere strongly for reasons which have nothing to do with national politics. The antidotes to corruption are strong and independent party organisations (not parties formed as 'fronts' by magnates who remain outside the organisation) and good electoral administration. These things are necessary to the modernisation of a state for other reasons besides their importance in the electoral system: this perhaps is the best reason for hoping that in political development better electoral practice goes closely with better management of government in other respects.

3. Made elections

But if administrative organisation is better developed than party organisation—as in many European countries in the nineteenth century—the tendency is for the administration to 'make' the elections. There were some traces of this in the practice of elections in England before reform, but the influence of the Crown though substantial was never paramount. Electoral 'manufacture' flourished especially under the liberalised European monarchies of the nineteenth century; regimes dominant in societies where there was much freedom of public expression, but little experience of electoral organisation. These monarchies (and the Third Republic in France at first followed this example) inherited excellent bureaucratic organisations; they believed (not without some reason) that there was no alternative regime except revolutionary dictatorship; yet they had neither power nor inclination to suppress opposition completely. Extreme radicals were dealt with very severely; milder opponents remained within 'the pale of the constitution'; but the resources of the administration were used to ensure that government candidates obtained a very large majority in the elected assembly.

The 'manufacture' of elections is not technically a difficult operation; at practically every point described in this book officials can intervene to bias the system in favour of one set of candidates and against others. Elections made skilfully are made by minor interventions at a large number of points, not by brutal interposition at a few. The officials do not block all opposition by sabotaging the nomination of all candidates out of sympathy with the regime; they merely twist matters a little in delimiting constituencies, making up the register, dealing with nominations, giving facilities for the campaign, conducting the poll, enquiring into disputed cases. The sum of these things should be enough to keep the government in power, unless it has involved the nation in disaster, and they do not incur the odium of dictatorship.

This at least was the theory of electoral management. In practice, the system has always broken down, sooner or later, because if the government in power failed in its policy, and was seen to fail, there was no alternative to it except turmoil; the 'loyal' opposition was inexperienced in government, all other political leaders were in gaol, and the public had grown suspicious of the show of democracy.

4. *Elections by acclamation*

Hence, since the time of Napoleon I, more resolute dictators have pushed on beyond the stage of made elections to the paradox of 'unfree' elections, elections in which the voters have no choice. In a Napoleonic or Nazi plebiscite, in a Russian election, there is only one candidate, the dictator or the party. The possibility is held out to voters that they may dissent by abstaining or by casting a negative vote, but every step is taken to see that this possibility does not really exist. No one believes in the secrecy of the ballot, the fate of known opponents of the regime is terrible, the whole population is mustered to attend the poll, and its votes can be depended upon—it is probably unnecessary to fake the count, though this is of course within the power of a totalitarian regime. The result is that an election ceases to be a public act of choice and becomes a public act of acclamation. Zealous servants of the regime push voting statistics to unheard of levels—99% of the electorate voting, 99% of the votes in favour of the government; such figures condemn themselves in the sight of anyone who knows anything about electoral administration. There remains something which is called an election, and which possesses some of the trappings of an election, such as electoral cards, polling booths and voting papers: but which belongs in substance to the category not of elections but of public demonstrations, such as May Day processions and Nuremberg rallies. To quote (at secondhand) from an East German official: 'The actual voting is of no importance. It has all the inevitability of a marriage ceremony. The courting of the bride has been done.'

In Europe, the system in this extreme form has been used only by Hitler, and it is unlikely that there are parallels elsewhere. It is a form of government which has no merits, not even tactical ones: the pretence of unanimity deceives no one who does not wish to be deceived, yet the maintenance of electoral forms keeps alive the notion that the regime is a matter for the people's choice, and in that sense is dangerous to dictators. Dictators not so convinced of the supremacy of the big lie in politics (Mussolini for instance and Franco) have avoided elections of any kind, and have looked elsewhere for arguments about their right to govern. Others have introduced the right to choose between approved candidates (Portugal, for instance, and Nasser's Egypt), but not between rival organisations, and in Communist countries this exclusion of rival organisations is a matter of principle.

Current Marxist doctrine bases the Party's right to govern on historical necessity, since it is the vanguard of the proletariat, the governing class in the stage of transition to Communism. The Party cannot admit a rival without self-contradiction, and a state which admits more parties than one cannot be (under present orthodoxy) a truly Marxist regime. It may be accepted and blessed by Russia as a 'popular democracy', a step in the right direction: or it may be rejected as heretical. That is a matter of tactics; principle on this issue is un-bending.

Nevertheless, there is room for compromise, since the Party's claim to pre-eminence is valid only if it truly understands and leads the proletariat, and it is therefore desirable that the people should have some freedom of expression in its relations with the Party. The Russian doctrine is that candidates for public office should be pre-selected by discussions under the guidance of the Party in Trade Unions, collective farms, cultural organisations and other non-political public bodies. In the end only one candidate is put forward for each seat; but (if the system is played fairly) he is put forward in a representative capacity, as some-one known to a good many people in the constituency, and it is probable that candidates are drawn from a number of nominating bodies in turn. It has never been possible to make a serious and detailed study of Russian elections, but there is strong reason to disbelieve the official account; after all, election to a Soviet Assembly is election to an honour and privilege, not to a position of power, and the Party (if it is wise) sees that honours go round in a way approved by the public. There is indeed no theoretical reason why the electorate should not be offered a choice between candidates, so long as candidates and electorate are denied all opportunities for organisation outside the control of the Party.

But such a compromise would be difficult to maintain, and some of its problems were illustrated by the Polish elections of January 1957

Poland was then in the form of a popular democracy: that is to say there still existed parties other than the Communist Party, though these were no more than 'rumps' of superannuated politicians, playing no effective part in government. The problem of 'the thaw' in Poland arose not from the existence of non-Communist parties, but from division within the party itself, between those who supported Russia at all costs and those who thought that the Party could only maintain a position of leadership in Poland if it recognised the existence of Polish problems and Polish national feeling. After a complicated train of events, this division within the Party brought back into power as Party Secretary a certain Gomulka, who had been in prison as an opponent of the Russian line, and his appointment was followed in January 1957 by elections of a very peculiar kind. Since Poland is a popular democracy the regime is not that of the Communist Party, but that of a National Front, dominated by the Party (known in Poland as the Polish United Workers Party), but including the Peasant Party, the Democratic Party, and various national organisations of Trade Unions, youth clubs, and so on. A popular democracy might conduct elections by acclamation, and in that event no more candidates would be nominated than there were seats to be filled. But Gomulka went beyond this, in that his newly-made electoral law permitted the number of candidates to exceed the number of seats to be filled by not more than two-thirds: that is to say, there might be five candidates for a three-member constituency, six or seven for one of four members, and so on. Voters might express a choice either by returning the list intact, which was a vote for those at the head of the list, or by striking names off and thus voting only for those whose names remained, or by abstaining, since 50% abstention would invalidate an election. The candidates on the lists were pre-selected by consultative committees of the political parties, dominated by Communists, and it is to be assumed that those openly hostile to the regime were eliminated, and that those preferred by the regime headed the lists. But of the candidates on the lists (723 for 459 seats) about 360 were Communist, 180 Peasant Party, 70 Democratic Party, and 114 non-party. The electorate were thus given some clue as to the general political tendency of the individuals put before them, and in addition rumour credited individual Communist candidates with affiliation to one faction or another within the Party. It was not therefore difficult to express a real choice between policies as well as between personalities: and observers agree that (apart from a certain amount of administrative confusion) the elections were honestly conducted.

The results were not easy to assess, but the limited statistics available in the West indicated real variations in the attitudes of voters to candidates of different tendencies, and they were widely construed as a victory for a strange alliance between Polish Communism and the

Catholic Church in Poland. Were these then 'free elections'? Were they 'elections' at all? Do they not belong to the category of 'public opinion poll' rather than to that of 'choice'? Governments are of course influenced by opinion polls, they even organise them for their own purposes, but it is generally taken to be a sign not of freedom but of servitude if the government in power takes a great deal of trouble to find out what people think about it. Public opinion has approved the activities of the disguised Caliph Haroun-el-Raschid in Baghdad, but not those of 'Cooper's snoopers' (the pollsters of the Ministry of Information) in Britain during the war.

5. Conclusion

These questions are worth asking, but cannot be answered. They serve here to direct attention to two questions outside the scope of this book.

The first is that it is not easy to find a definition which will distinguish between an election and a mere expression of opinion. Probably most of us feel that there is a difference between 'opinion' and 'consent'. All governments, if not foolishly conducted, have regard to opinion; democratic governments rest on consent. A public opinion poll is not an election or a plebiscite, even if governments have regard to its results. One can distinguish between 'freedom' and 'unfreedom' in an opinion poll as well as in an election, by various criteria suggested in this book: but one can distinguish 'election' from 'opinion' only by saying that the former binds the government constitutionally, the latter does not. That is to say, an election is an expression of choice which is accepted as constitutionally binding: it confers legitimate authority. Beyond this one cannot go without an enquiry into the nature of authority and the nature of political obligation.

The second point is that if the notion of consent by elections is once introduced it works within a system like a grain of mustard seed, which is 'the least of all seeds, but when it is grown it is the greatest of herbs, and becometh a tree, so that the birds of the air come and lodge in the branches thereof'. At the time of writing, the fate of the Polish Seym is uncertain, and matters may go either way. But limited and partial freedom in elections at once raised in Poland the question of the status of the elected body: there is a principle of legitimacy at work challenging the legitimacy of the Party, and the former is likely to expand until it meets too great an obstacle. Similarly, in colonial territories outside the Russian orbit, the introduction of any elected members into an assembly at once raises the question of their superiority in status to nominated members: and members elected on a wider suffrage challenge members elected on a narrower one. While the current runs this way, in favour of popular consent to government, it can scarcely be checked by counter-arguments about the need to keep government in the hands of 'civilised' people, or about the pre-eminence of skilled administration in the modern world. Almost everything in this book has indicated the practical limits of consent: the mathematics of representation are puzzling, no elections are possible without reliable administration, the effective range of choice is limited by the necessity for decision. This line of thought suggests that a satisfactory theory of government must include other elements besides a theory of consent: respect must be paid to tradition, to skill, to establish economic expectations. But none of these things can stand alone, and they can fight only a rearguard action in debate if a public demand for free elections has arisen and remains unsatisfied. It is this which keeps the question of elections at the centre of politics everywhere, in spite of long perplexity and much disappointment.

BIBLIOGRAPHY

1. ELECTORAL SYSTEMS IN GENERAL
There is no book which covers electoral qualifications and electoral management as well as electoral systems.

Voting systems
Enid Lakeman and J. D. Lambert: *Voting in Democracies* (London, 1955) is reliable in spite of the authors' special interest in advocating the single transferable vote.
This may be balanced by:—
    F. A. Hermens: *Democracy v. Anarchy. A Study of Proportional Representation* (Notre Dame Univ. Press, 1941), a more extreme exposition of the opposite point of view.
    J. Hogan: *Election and Representation* (Cork, 1945) is more moderate.

Parties and elections
The main comparative works, stimulating but not always reliable in detail, are:—
    M. Duverger et al: 'The Influence of Electoral Systems on Political Life': *International Social Science Bulletin,* summer 1951 (Vol. III, No. 2).
    M. Duverger: *Political Parties* (trans. B. and R. North: London, 1954).

2. THE UNITED KINGDOM

(a) *The growth of the system*
The history of electoral reform in Britain throws a good deal of light both on the technical problems that are encountered in the making of electoral systems and on the arguments about representation that may be used by politicians.
    E. and A. Porritt: *The Unreformed House of Commons* (London, 1903).
    C. Seymour: *Electoral Reform in England and Wales* (New Haven, U.S.A., 1915).
    H. L. Morris: *Parliamentary Franchise Reform in England from 1885 to 1918* (New York, 1921).
    D. E. Butler: *The Electoral System in Britain, 1915 to 1951* (London, 1953).
    B. Keith-Lucas: *The English Local Government Franchise* (Oxford, 1952).

(b) *Present electoral law*
    A. N. Schofield: *Parliamentary Elections* (London, 1955).
    A. N. Schofield: *Local Government Elections* (London, 1954).

(c) *Electoral practice*
Perhaps a general reader will best grasp the problems of continuity and change by comparing an account of an old-style election with an account of an election today: selecting from:—
    (i) J. E. Neale: *The Elizabethan House of Commons* (London, 1949).
    E. G. Forrester: *Northamptonshire County Elections and Electioneering, 1695–1832* (London, 1941).
    R. J. Robson: *The Oxfordshire Election of 1754* (London, 1949).
    Charles Dickens: *Pickwick Papers* (published in 1837): Chap. XIII on the Eatanswill Election.
    H. G. Nicholas: *To the Hustings* (London, 1956).

(ii) R. B. MacCallum and Alison Readman: *The British General Election of 1945* (London, 1947).

H. G. Nicholas: *The British General Election of 1950* (London, 1951).

D. E. Butler: *The British General Election of 1951* (London, 1952).

D. E. Butler: *The British General Election of 1955* (London, 1956).

S. B. Chrimes et al: *The General Election in Glasgow, February, 1950* (Glasgow, 1950).

3. FRANCE

(a) *Electoral systems*

The methods of voting and of allocating seats are described historically in:—

P. Campbell: *French Electoral Systems and Elections, 1789–1956* (London, 1958).

The best account in English of the electoral systems used since 1945, in relation to the party system, is to be found in:—

P. Williams: *Politics in Post-War France* (London, 1954).

(b) *Electoral practices*

Electoral practices in the nineteenth and early twentieth centuries are described in:—

A. Pilenco: *Les Moeurs Électorales—Régime Censitaire* (Paris, 1928).

A. Pilenco: *Les Moeurs du Suffrage Universel* (Paris, 1930).

The election of 1956 has been the object of detailed studies suitable for the specialist rather than for the general reader:—

M. Duverger et al: *Les Elections du 2 janvier 1956* (Paris, 1957).

H. G. Nicholas et al: 'The French Elections' in *Political Studies*, Oxford, June and October, 1956 (Vol. 6, Nos. 2 and 3).

4. GERMANY

A comprehensive account of German electoral law and practice in 1953 is given in:—

J. K. Pollock et al: *German Democracy at Work* (Ann Arbor, U.S.A., 1955).

5. U.S.A.

(a) *Parties and elections*

Literature about elections in the U.S.A. is concerned less with voting systems than with the relations between party machines, the society in which they exist, and the management of elections. The general nature of American elections is described in the many general text-books on American government. A number of text-books deal specifically with parties and elections, emphasising generally the problems of politicians and voters, rather than those of administrators. For instance:—

C. E. Merriam and H. Gosnell: *American Political Parties* (New York, 1949).

V. O. Key: *Politics, Parties, and Pressure Groups* (New York, 1952).

V. O. Key: *Southern Politics* (New York, 1949).

These books will guide readers to the vast literature on parties, politicians, and elections in the U.S.A.

(b) *Electoral machinery*

Among the works dealing with aspects of the electoral system are:—

B. M. Bernard: *Election Laws of the 48 States* (New York, 1950).

S. D. Albright: *The American Ballot* (New York, 1942).

P. T. David et al: *Presidential Nominating Politics in 1952* (5 vols., Baltimore, U.S.A., 1956).

6. OTHER WESTERN COUNTRIES

The general reader will find very little material available in English. Most text-books on the government of individual countries devote a chapter or two to parties and elections.

7. SOVIET UNION

There is a short book based on material available in the U.S.A.:—

G. B. Carson: *Electoral Practices in the U.S.S.R.* (New York, 1956).

Communist electoral theories and practices are described in the various text-books on Soviet government, e.g.:—

D. J. R. Scott: *Russian Political Institutions* (London, 1957).

M. Fainsod: *How Russia is Ruled* (Cambridge, U.S.A., 1953).

8. AFRICAN AND ASIAN COUNTRIES

No systematic study has yet been made of the large-scale adoption of electoral systems in Africa and Asia. There is a collection of electoral laws in

H. C. M. Davis (Ed.): *Constitutions, Electoral Laws, and Treaties of States in the Near and Middle East* (London, 1947).

Texts on the government of Ceylon and Japan describe the countries with the longest electoral experience. See particularly:—

S. Namasivayam: *The Legislatures of Ceylon 1928–1948* (London, 1951).

C. Yanaga: *Japanese People and Politics* (London, 1956).

There is a growing literature of government reports and independent studies of the mass electorates enfranchised since 1951. Perhaps the report of most interest to the general reader is that on the most gigantic experiment yet made:—

Report on the First General Election in India, 1951–52 (Election Commission, India, 1955).

See also:—

S. V. Kogekar et al: *Reports on the Indian General Election, 1951–52* (Popular Book Depot, Bombay).

W. H. Morris-Jones: *Parliament in India* (London, 1957).

Some recent elections in Africa are described in:—

W. J. M. Mackenzie and K. E. Robinson (edd.): *Five Elections in Africa* (Oxford, 1958).

There are a number of useful articles in two accessible journals. Those in *Parliamentary Affairs* (London, 1948–date) will be of most interest to the general reader; they are:—

Ceylon: Autumn 1952, Summer 1956.

Gold Coast: Summer 1951, Autumn 1954.

India: Spring 1952, Summer 1953, Autumn 1953, Spring 1954.

Sudan: Summer 1954.

The specialist will be more interested in certain articles in *The Journal of African Administration* (London, 1949–date):—

Gold Coast: April 1951.
Nigeria: July 1952.
W. Nigeria: January 1957.

There is a general discussion of the problems of establishing free popular government in:—

W. I. Jennings: *The Approach to Self-Government* (London, 1956).

INDEX

181

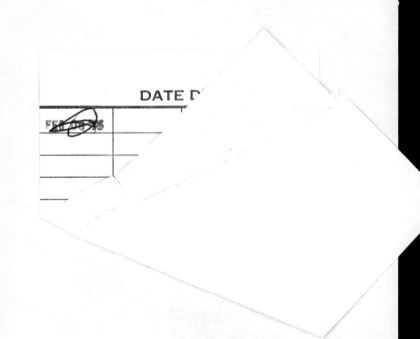

DATE D

FEB